BY THE GRACE OF GOD: I AM WHAT I AM
DR HAMILTON MOORE

By the Grace of God

I AM WHAT I AM

DR HAMILTON MOORE

ISBN 978-1-909751-58-3

Copyright © 2017 Dr Hamilton Moore

The rights of Dr Hamilton Moore to be identified as the author of this book have been asserted by them in accordance with the Copyright, Designs and Patents Act 1988.

All rights reserved. No part of this book may be reproduced, stored in a retrieval system, or transmitted, in any form or by any means, electronic, mechanical, photocopying, recording, or otherwise, without the prior written permission of the publisher.

The entire proceeds of this book will be dedicated to the
Life and Learning Fund for Pastors and Students in Romania.

Further copies can be obtained from dr.hamilton.moore@gmail.com *or*
Church Office, Coleraine Baptist Church, Abbey Street, Coleraine, BT52 1EX.

Printed by J.C. Print Ltd.   email: info@jcprint.net

DEDICATION

*To my mother, Jean (née Wilkinson) Moore,
who asked for me from the Lord
and then gave me back to him
to live for his glory*

DR HAMILTON MOORE

The Letters to Timothy and Titus

Missional Texts
from a
Great Missionary
Statesman

Also published by Dr Hamilton Moore

The Letters to Timothy and Titus.
Missional Texts from a Great Missionary Statesman
A commentary by Dr. Hamilton Moore.
Hardback Cover.
Over 300 pages.

These Letters are of vital importance in any study of the New Testament. In them the Apostle Paul encourages, warns and teaches Timothy and Titus and in fact through them, the churches in Ephesus and Crete. The emphasis on being faithful to the truth and sharing the gospel through local Church witness and Christian lifestyle is as relevant now in the twenty-first century as it was in the first.

I hope this book will bring challenges to the church today to continue by these means to further the mission of God. It is primarily aimed at providing a resource for busy pastors, enabling them to understand how one can interpret the biblical text faithfully and practically for the benefit of the people of God.

Hamilton Moore

All proceeds from the distribution of this book will be used for the "Life and Learning Fund" for Pastors and Students in the land of Romania.

Book available from:
Most Christian Bookshops in Northern Ireland or by email from
dr.hamilton.moore@gmail.com

FOREWORD

'Desire that your life count for something great! Long for your life to have eternal significance. Want this! Don't coast through life without a passion'. ('Don't waste your life' by John Piper first published in 2003)

YOU HAVE IN YOUR HANDS the story of one who for more than fifty years has lived his life as Piper exhorts. Books that recount the gracious working of God through a man's lifetime in ministry are always worth reading. But this book is all the more valuable because that man is Hamilton Moore. He is not one who seeks the limelight, nor is he flamboyant by nature, so he is not as widely known as other powerful evangelists of Ulster. Some of those greatly used by God in the past were larger than life characters and indeed several of them were early role models for the author of this book. But here is the account of one whose life of service for the Lord has quietly, faithfully and yet so powerfully been of eternal significance – and only through the Grace of God.

Here you will meet a boy whose mother persevered in prayer for a son so that she might give him back to the Lord. Here is the story of a teenage evangelist who very early knew the love of God that compels and the call of God that propels. This account opens a window on a lifetime of experience and wisdom and passion; a ministry of evangelism, of church planting, of shepherding God's people. This is the story of a man gifted by God for College ministry, pouring himself into the lives of young men and women who would continue the task of evangelising the world.

Although this book looks back over fifty years of service, in the providence of God Hamilton's best years may not be behind him. He has a dream that even the 'retirement' years of his life will be of eternal significance; a dream summed up by the psalmist: 'The righteous ... still bear fruit in old age ... to declare that the Lord is upright' Psalm 92:12-15.

After his lifetime service for God, we could understand if Hamilton was minded to take life easy and enjoy walks and picnics in the delightful scenic area in which he lives in Northern Ireland. But God has graciously endowed him with health and vigour and has placed deep within his heart a dream of continued service far beyond these shores. And to help make that dream a reality, the Lord has given him another dreamer: his wife Shirley is as passionate about serving the Lord as he is. Romania's future will be the richer because of their commitment and sacrifice.

This book is not merely an autobiography but a rich account of evangelical life in Ulster at a time when halls and tents and churches were filled by people wanting to hear the gospel. It is also a book full of helpful teaching as, again and again Hamilton the pastor/ teacher / lecturer takes time to explain lessons learned and offer guidance and advice. That teenage evangelist more than fifty years later is still passionate about sharing the gospel, so expect to read the way of salvation clearly presented here. These pages also give a challenging insight into the needy mission-field of Romania, the land of Hamilton's adoption and they reveal something of the burden the Lord has laid upon his heart for the Romanian people. As you read, you will be challenged. You will ask yourself, 'Do I truly desire that by the grace of God my life might be of eternal significance?'

Pastor David McFarland
Lurgan, N. Ireland

A WORD FROM THE AUTHOR

FINALLY THE DAY ARRIVED! It was Saturday 24th September 1966; the special day I had longed for and looked forward to for a few years, because I knew that God was calling me to dedicate my life in total surrender to seek the lost. I terminated my employment with F.C. Glasgow's of Newtownards that day to walk the path of full-time service for God. That was 50 years ago. This book is the story of the Lord's grace over all the 70 years of my life and particularly a record of how God guided, enabled and used his servant over the past 50.

In 2 Tim. 4v7 Paul claims 'I have finished my course'. Beginning on the road to Damascus, he had gone on throughout his life in the path that God had mapped out for him to that moment. Similarly God has had a path mapped out for my life and I have sought to follow it. It is amazing how in seeking to 'keep in step' with God on that path of service, he has led me from the little village of Ballyhalbert in Co. Down, Northern Ireland to serve first as an evangelist, then as pastor of a number of churches, also as Principal of the Irish Baptist College and finally to establish the work of Tell Romania. Now his purpose is for me to become a missionary with my wife Shirley in the needy land of Romania, preaching in cities like Suceava, Targu Mures, Cluj; teaching in Emanuel Baptist University, Oradea, even to help plant a church in a village like Odoreu in the north-west of the country. This book will chart that course in three main parts. In Part One, I will tell of my early life and the ministry God gave me largely in Northern Ireland; Part Two, will speak of opportunities given to serve him in the needy land of Romania. Part Three will ask the question Why this Story? It will challenge you to be involved in God's mission in the world – Romania or wherever he wills.

Why write this account of my life and ministry? Those who know me will appreciate I am not one to boast. Basically there are a number of reasons.

First, that God may be glorified through the record of all his dealings with me. Recalling the past has brought home to me afresh the kindness, great mercy and grace of God which I have received down through all the years of my life. It moves me personally to call out in praise to him. 'Now to the King eternal, immortal, invisible, to God who alone is wise, be honour and glory for ever and ever. Amen!' (1 Timothy 1v17).

Second, that you may be encouraged through seeing how God has worked in an ordinary life in what I would consider are extraordinary ways.

Third, that you may benefit from the teaching sections, and prayerfully consider giving your book to another (or buy a second copy) because of its 'gospel' content.

Fourthly, to make you aware of the great need in the land of Romania so that you might pray in a more informed way for the country and the work of the kingdom in which we and others are involved, Emanuel University with staff and students, and in the local churches highlighted in this book.

Finally, to remind you that we are all involved in the mission of God and so to challenge you to respond personally to God in allowing him to be God in your life so that you can be his instrument when and where he wills.

The book is dedicated to the one who greatly influenced my early life – my mother. She prayed for me before I was born, prayed *with* me in my formative years and gave me such an example of godliness. She was a blessing to so many in Ballyhalbert where she lived – a true mother in Israel. My special thanks also go to my loving wife Shirley who has helped me so much in recording the story of these years; to my friend Pastor David McFarland for his unwavering support and dutiful assistance concerning content and presentation and to Mrs Margaret Rodgers for her attention to detail in editing. The quotations from the Scriptures are taken from the King James Version unless otherwise stated.

ABBREVIATIONS

AD	After Death
BC	Before Christ
BD	Bachelor of Divinity
BUOI	Baptist Union of Ireland
CWU	Christian Workers Union Hall
DD	Doctor of Divinity
ESV	English Standard Version
GmbH	Gesellschaft mit beschränkter Haftung
GNP	Gross National Product
IBC	Irish Baptist College, Northern Ireland
IVP	Inter Varsity Press
kms	kilometres
MA	Massachusetts
MI	Michigan
MTh	Master of Theology
NT	New Testament
OT	Old Testament
PhD	Doctor of Philosophy
Phm	Philemon
RKFDV	Reichskommissar für die Festigung deutschen Volkstums
SGA UK	Slavic Gospel Association, United Kingdom

CONTENTS

Foreword	9
A Word from the Author	11
Abbreviations	13
PART ONE: Hamilton Moore – Evangelist; Pastor; Principal of Irish Baptist College	19
(A) Hamilton Moore – Evangelist	19
Saved by Grace	19
Excursus: The Lord's Return	20
My Godly Mother	21
The Early Years	22
'Whom the Lord loveth…' Hebrews 12v6	26
Excursus: Motives for Evangelism	29
Amy Carmichael's Dream	32
The Work of an Evangelist	34
'From This Day…' Haggai 2v19	38
Excursus: Preaching – Content and Manner	40
People's Hall, Portavogie	47
Knocknagoney Mission	48
South Derry	49
Magherafelt Baptist Church	53

(B) Hamilton Moore – Pastor 55
    54 Moneymore Road 56
    On the Road Again 59

Excursus: Memorial Service 62
    Fellowship in the Gospel and Glenarm Church Plant 66
    Monkstown Baptist Church 70
    Student Days and Glenarm 71
    Is that the Phone? 74
    How you have grown! 76
    Ministry in Magherafelt 77
    The Pieces of the Jigsaw fit! 81

(C) Hamilton Moore – Principal of IBC 83
    Principal with New Team Members 83
    Daddy's Boys 83
    Castlereagh Baptist 84
    A Workman seeking not to be Ashamed 85

Excursus: Basic Principles of Interpretation 85
    Romania Comes to Belfast and Vice Versa 87
    The Comfort of Psalm 16 88
    Gideon's Fleece 90
    Developments at IBC 94

PART TWO: Hamilton Moore – Missionary;
Adjunct Professor; Founder of Tell Romania 97

(A) Hamilton Moore – Missionary in Romania –
  Land of Pain and the Power of God 97
  The Bread Basket of Europe 97
  The Ethnic Germans in Romania 99
  The Romanian Jews 100
  The Roma Communities 102
  Revival among the Roma 103
  Satu Mare and Odoreu 104
  Orphanages and Orphans 106
  The Caminul Felix Community and Casa Grace 107
  Communism and Ceausescu 108
  Richard Wurmbrand (1909-2001) 109
  Revival in Oradea 113
  Liviu Olah 114
  Paul Negrut 116
  From Belfast to Romania 118

(B) Hamilton Moore – Adjunct Professor of Emanuel 118
  Among the Five Percent 118
  Emanuel University 119
  'Two are better than one …' 122
  Compelled by love alone 124
  Shirley's Blogs 126

Excursus: The Hospice Leaflet 136

(C) Hamilton Moore – Founder of Tell Romania 139
  tellromania.org 139

PART THREE: Why This Story? 143
    What Paul Wrote 2 Tim. 4v1-13 143
    What Jesus Said John 9v4 147

Bibliography 151

Websites 153

Endnotes 155

PART ONE: Hamilton Moore – Evangelist; Pastor; Principal of IBC

(A) Hamilton Moore – Evangelist

IN PAUL'S FIRST EPISTLE he can emphasise that his calling as a preacher goes back to God and his marvellous grace: Galatians 1v15-16 states, 'When it pleased God, who separated me from my mother's womb, and called me by his grace, To reveal his son in me, that I might preach him among the Gentiles...' My call to preach also finds its source in the gracious purposes of God who first set his love upon me, in grace drew me to himself and planned my way.

Saved by Grace
True, my conversion was of God but he used two others as instruments in his hand – my mother and a young man sharing his testimony. I often went with my parents (Hamilton & Jean) to the Gospel Hall in Ballyhalbert in the Ards Peninsula on Sunday evenings. On one occasion a Mr. Wilson and his son, whom I learned many years later was called Henry, came from Donaghadee to take the meeting. Henry led the first part and giving his testimony, told how God awakened and saved him. He was one of nine children; four boys (he was the youngest) and five girls. His parents and others in the family were converted but he was not. He realised that the Lord Jesus Christ was coming again; yet he was not prepared. Neither was I.

I knew my father, mother and sister (May) were saved but I had no personal assurance of this. I remember my mother speaking to me the next morning about my need. If I came to the Lord Jesus he would say to me as he said to Moses, 'I will do this thing also that thou hast spoken; for thou hast found grace in my sight, and I know thee by name', Exodus 33v17. But if I did not come to him, one day he would solemnly say, 'I tell you, I know you not whence ye are; Depart from me, all ye workers of iniquity', Luke 13v27. We got on our knees in the little kitchen in High Street, Ballyhalbert and as my mother prayed for me I said yes to him in my heart and I knew that he had accepted me. It was an amazing moment. My mother was not finished but took me to John 6v37, 'All that the Father giveth me shall come to me; and him that cometh to me I will in no wise cast out'. The Lord's promise was sure and I was able to rest upon it. It was Monday 18th February 1952 at 9 am. She encouraged me to note that special life-changing day in the front of my bible and it is still there, written in a child's hand. It is of course the promise of the God 'that cannot lie', Titus 1v2. And I no longer had any fear of the coming of the Lord.

Excursus: The Lord's Return

The coming of the Lord is sure. It has often been stated that in the 280 chapters of the New Testament there are no less than 318 references to it; one verse in every 25 focuses upon the Lord's return. One cannot explain away the promise of his coming as fulfilled when a believer dies. In John 21v22-23 Jesus says to Peter concerning John, 'If I will that he tarry till I come, what is that to thee? Follow thou me'. We are told that because of that statement the brethren were considering that John would not die! He would rather remain alive until Jesus would come! Again, the idea that the clear statements about his return could be explained as some kind of spiritual coming e.g., when right conquers wrong or when some great blessing is poured upon the church is ruled out by the use of the word *Parousia* which signifies personal presence, the presence of the king. 1 Thess. 4v16 reveals 'The Lord HIMSELF shall descend…' and in Acts 1v11 the angels affirm 'This same Jesus which is taken up from you into heaven, shall SO COME IN LIKE MANNER as you have seen him go into heaven'. This requires that he return LITERALLY, BODILY, ACTUALLY, not in some spiritual sense only. The question now remains – are you ready for that coming?

So we can affirm that the coming of the Lord is an uncertain certainty; certain as to the fact, uncertain as to the time. His coming will be 'in the twinkling of an eye', 1 Cor. 15 v52; like 'a thief in the night' 1 Thess. 5v2. Think of the teaching of Jesus about the moment the door is shut. Those who have been careless and procrastinated will cry, 'Lord, Lord, open unto us… we have eaten and drunk in thy presence and thou hast taught in our streets' Luke 13v25-26. They know the language 'Lord, Lord'; they have sat in his presence and listened to his teaching. But although they are familiar with the language, knowing the hymns, the texts, the truth, although they have sat in church in his presence and listened to the teaching they are STILL OUTSIDE! Isaiah 55v6 reminds us, 'Seek ye the Lord WHILE he may be found' – for one day he will no more be found – 'call ye upon him WHILE he is near' – for one day he will be no longer near.

My Godly Mother
My sister was twenty when I was born. My mother and father waited many years for a son. In 1 Sam. 1v27-28 we read of Elkanah and Hannah who had no children. Hannah announced, 'For this child I prayed; and the Lord hath given me my petition which I asked of him: Therefore also I have lent him to the Lord; as long as he liveth …' My mother told me that God impressed this passage upon her heart when she first asked God for a son. I learned about this commitment when I talked to her of my sense of call to go out in faith to preach. When I was born she was over fifty years of age.

My mother's bible, a treasured possession, contains (in many places) the capitals T&P, 'tried and proven'. These letters would be in the margin where there were promises which were made real in her experience. One such promise was Proverbs 4v12, 'When thou goest thy steps shall not be straitened; and when thou runnest thou shall not stumble'. On this occasion she had to enter Musgrave Park Hospital to have an operation on her hip joint. Mr Withers informed her that if she agreed to the surgery she would have to lie in plaster throughout the summer until the bone grew. In fact she would have to learn to walk again when she finally would get out of bed. God gave her the promise that she would not just walk again but run! She would often in the months to follow, ask my father to stop when they got out of the car. She would then run up the footpath, turn around and laugh.

The reality of her faith and godliness was known in the little village. One occasion I recall was when the local Postmistress took seriously ill and it became clear she would not recover. My mother, who was well known in the village for her Christian witness, went to see her and was readily welcomed. My mother opened her bible, read to her and had the joy of pointing her to Christ. The whole village soon knew of it.

I was preaching at the funeral of a dear lady from Carnalbanagh, Glenarm, (Mrs Martha McCalmont), in the Glenarm cemetery when my mother was called home (14th August 1976), passing peacefully into the presence of the Lord. She had had an operation for cancer many years earlier but kept from me the reality of the fact that it had returned until she was taken into Newtownards Hospital. She herself – when I went first to see her gently and lovingly told me of the seriousness of her illness. I had only a few precious days with her; our time together was short, but very special.

The Early Years

My early life was spent in both Ballyhalbert and Belfast. My mother gave birth to me on 12th September 1945 and as a family we lived in 10 Artana Street, Ormeau Road. My parents were faithful members of Great Victoria Street Baptist Church during the time of Pastor Henderson. My father was a bus conductor, but suffered from asthma and was advised to leave the city smog to live in a healthier atmosphere. Ballyhalbert was certainly that! The smell of the sea, the soft summer breeze and the winter gales were indeed a very different climate. It was the opportunity to work with his father (also called Hamilton) a tailor, living in Clifton House, High Street which brought all four of us there. Later he went on to be employed by James Gillies, Royal Avenue, Belfast. He became a Master Tailor winning various silver and gold medals in the trade and in fact largely managing the business. The village was an idyllic place to live, the Sandylands beach at the little harbour, where I could swim, catch fish with a piece of string and a safety pin, the old Aerodrome (from the second world war), the moat and dolmen overlooking the houses of Harbour Road, the open countryside with various farms where you could gather potatoes and help reap the harvest on the combine harvester. The quiet and uneventful main street with only two shops was the perfect playground where one could play and cycle.

But it appeared it was difficult for my mother to settle. We made several trips back to live in different parts of Belfast; residing in Ardcarn Drive,

Dundonald, Beersbridge Road, Donard Street (worshipping again in Great Victoria Street Baptist Church, where I attended Sunday School and accompanied my parents to all the Sunday services) and of course returning to different houses in Ballyhalbert, no less than three in High Street, then No 1 Moat Road, and finally, Victoria Gardens. God was preparing me not to put my roots down too deeply. As a pastor I would be moving from church to church; more so in the weeks and months away from home as an evangelist and finally spending years travelling back and forward to Romania.

Schooling for the young Hamilton 3rd began in Ballyhalbert Primary School, moving to Ballywalter Primary School, where pupils received extra tuition on Saturdays for the 11 plus then on to Regent House Grammar School, Newtownards. I recall the mornings getting ready for the early bus, my godly mother never failed to open the word of God to read and pray that God would be with me. How this spiritual influence in those early years has lived with me throughout my lifetime. Yet I must confess that I did not really take a stand for the Lord in school but largely kept my light hidden – it was 'under a bushel' rather than 'on a candlestick', Matt. 5v15.

Yet I can remember how in my early teenage years God's word to his young servant Jeremiah would fill my mind. Jeremiah 1v4-10:

Then the word of the Lord came unto me, saying:
'Before I formed thee in the belly, I knew thee; and before thou camest forth out of the womb I sanctified thee, and I ordained thee a prophet unto the nations'. Then said I, 'Ah, Lord God! Behold, I cannot speak: for I am a child'. But the Lord said unto me, 'Say not, 'I am a child: For thou shalt go to all that I shall send thee, and whatsoever I command thee thou shalt speak. Be not afraid of their faces: for I am with thee to deliver thee', saith the Lord. Then the Lord put forth his hand, and touched my mouth. And the Lord said unto me, 'Behold, I have put my words in thy mouth. See, I have this day set thee over the nations and over the kingdoms, to root out, and to pull down, and to destroy, and to throw down, to build, and to plant'.

I wondered at times if God had possibly in his grace 'ordained' me to preach although 'a child' like Jeremiah. Was he saying to me 'Be not afraid of their faces ... Behold, I have put my words in thy mouth ...' I must 'root out and ... pull down', to show people that they were only sinners with nothing to commend them to God. Then 'to build, and to plant', with the great truths of his precious word.

It was also during those early years that I became friendly with a boy a few years older than myself, Harvey Shaw. Harvey was to go on to be effectively used as a great evangelist and the Pastor of Lurgan Elim, then of Killicomaine Baptist Church and served a term as President of the Association of Baptist Churches in Ireland. Harvey organised a football team for a couple of years – Ballyhalbert United, 'the reds', and when I was around thirteen I played at right back. With Harvey as Manager we even won a couple of Trophies in the Lower Ards league! But of course my mother was anxious that I would know more spiritual influence in my life. At one point she began a Christian Endeavour in our own home. There are those who still remember the chain prayers in those meetings.

Harvey had also come to know the Lord – my mother's influence was strong yet again. Having both started in our sitting room on the Moat Road, Ballyhalbert, Harvey and I progressed to giving a little word in a Saturday night meeting held in the home of Mrs Pedelty on the Shore Road. I had prepared a sermon on John 3v16 all written down on pages of paper – it was over in ten minutes! But it was a start. Harvey had a great gift in preaching which was evident even in those early days. This meeting on a Saturday night was a source of real blessing for a number of young men in their twenties and thirties who were in other churches in the area, Glastry Methodist and Glastry Presbyterian Church. My father organised this meeting and it continued every Saturday night for many years. His faithfulness and dedication was evident, in that, during his time living in Donard Street, Belfast, he and my mother would make what was in those days, the long journey to Ballyhalbert.

The days passed quickly in Ballyhalbert and my mother encouraged me to settle in a spiritual home where I would find fellowship, and be taught the word of God. One Sunday morning we went to Ballyhalbert Gospel Hall or 'Bobby's hall' as the locals called it. Bobby McClements, a local farmer had been responsible for founding this hall in Ballyhalbert. He was a very godly brother, a man of prayer, who had many discouragements to face as he sought to maintain the witness in the village. His stance on welcoming to the Lord's table every visiting believer who desired to remember the Lord regardless of their own church affiliation meant that the hall was unique and effectively isolated among Gospel halls in the Ards Peninsula. Bobby once told me that at one point in his life he felt clearly called to the London City Mission, but he did not go. In grace God gave him another opportunity of service in Ballyhalbert. God is the God of the second chance.

This fellowship was to be my spiritual home for six years. Harvey also joined the hall and it led to the development of a 'Paul and Barnabas' type ministry as we preached in the local area in e.g., Cottage meetings (Mrs. Askin's little home at Dunover Corner, Ballywalter, Ballyfrenis Band Hall, People's Hall, Portavogie, Kircubbin CWU, Killaughy Mission Hall, Loughries Mission Hall, Donaghadee Gospel Hall, Scrabo Hall Newtownards, Holborn Hall, Bangor and beyond, even Carrickfergus Gospel Hall and Eden Hall. It has been rightly emphasised, that 'you cannot be a missionary across the sea until first of all you are a missionary across the street'. So we served God not only on platforms but in open airs and door to door. I recall the early days when we caught the vision of the late Ernie Allen of Every Home Crusade. We were able to gather together a huge group of young people to systematically put gospel literature into every home in the lower Ards.

I was baptised in Holborn Hall when I was 15 years of age. My attendance at the Hall in Ballyhalbert resulted in special years of spiritual growth and deepening understanding of God's word. Again, one highlight was that after the Prayer Meeting on a Saturday Night, a few of us always went to Hubert and Nancy Wilson's home a few doors from the hall. They were a special couple who were always open to the Lord's direction, expecting him to guide them daily. Often Hubert would tell me of special verses on their text calendar which often seemed so relevant to the changing situation of their daily lives. I learned from them to leave myself open to the Lord for daily guidance. Later in this book there will be more discussion about God's guidance, because there are different elements involved, not just the one mentioned here.

'Whom the Lord loveth ...' Hebrews 12v6

My school years had come to an end after Junior Certificate in Regent House School, Newtownards. A new system of assessment was being introduced,

GCE and A Level examinations. I had performed well at Junior Cert. and was moved up a year. I did not settle – I suppose I was not always in the top two or three as was the case in my first few years in Grammar School. The others were a year older. So I persuaded my parents to let me leave. I was really on the bottom rung of the ladder. I went to work in F.C. Glasgow's at £2.50 per week.

When I was approximately seventeen and a half I found that largely through the company of 'my friends' at work and elsewhere I was drifting away from the Lord. I started to miss meetings in the Hall, stopped reading and praying. I was at the top of a slippery slope. As Psalm 73v2 states 'As for me, my feet were almost gone; my steps had well nigh slipped'. Then God took a hold on my life. One Sunday, while driving my father's little A35, a car came right across the road at a T junction (approximately one mile outside Ballyhalbert) – I swerved violently but my car turned over and over and over but stayed on the road. Three of us climbed out shaken by not seriously hurt. I knew then that God in love (as the sub heading highlights) had intervened in my life. He had really said, 'That's it; no further; your life is mine. I have a work for you to do'. In the teaching in Hebrews 12v5-11, when God chastens his children, it is clear that there are three ways that we can respond to it. We can 'despise' it, refusing to heed or ignore what God is seeking to speak to us about; we can faint under it i.e., be 'discouraged' by it; or we can respect or be 'exercised' by it. On Monday night, returning from work, I knelt in my room with my bible open at Hosea 14. I confessed my coldness of heart, my waywardness, and sought the Lord. What a moment! The chapter became real in my life:

O Israel, return unto the Lord thy God; for thou hast fallen by thine iniquity. Take with you words, and turn to the Lord: say unto him, Take away all iniquity, and receive us graciously ... I will heal their backsliding, I will love them freely: for mine anger is turned away from him. I will be as the dew unto Israel ... Ephraim shall say, What have I to do any more with idols?

It was like a new salvation! In a short time I sensed deep within (also part of guidance) that God had a definite plan for my life; that I must give myself wholly to him and apply myself day by day (and sometimes late into the night) in preparation. The exhortation of Paul to his younger colleague Timothy powerfully affected me.

Let no man despise thy youth; but be thou an example of the believers, in word, in conversation, in charity, in spirit, in faith, in purity. Till I come, give attendance to reading, to exhortation, to doctrine. Neglect not the gift that is in thee ... Meditate on these things; give thyself wholly to them; that thy profiting may appear to all. Take heed unto thyself, and unto the doctrine; continue in them: for in doing this thou shalt both save thyself and them that hear thee, 1 Timothy 4v12-16.

I became quite radical in my dedication. Returning from work I would spend all of my time, as I mentioned, into the early hours studying the word of God. I travelled by car with my father every morning as far as Newtownards. He would leave me at the end of the canal on the Portaferry Road, where it entered Strangford Lough, and I would walk into the town. My father continued on to Belfast where he worked. I had one hour communing with the Lord as I walked into the town, talking and singing to him. Precious! I remember reading Psalm 73v22-25, then quoting these verses to the Lord as I was making them mine!

So foolish was I, and ignorant: I was as a beast before thee. Nevertheless I am continually before thee: thou hast holden me by my right hand. Thou shalt guide me with thy counsel, and afterward receive me to glory. Whom have I in heaven but thee? and there is none that I desire upon earth beside thee.

Then to sing those lovely words: 'I come to the garden alone, while the dew is still on the roses. And the voice I hear falling on my ear, the Son of God discloses. And **he walks with me and he talks with me. And he tells me I am his own. And the joy we share as we tarry there, none other has ever known'.** The presence of the Lord became so real in my experience! Within four years I was out in the work full-time!

Certain other verses were much in my mind in those days. Not only 1 Tim. 4v12-16 but 2 Tim. 4v5, 'Do the work of an evangelist'. But when could this begin? I was very young and how could I know the time for me to launch out to reach the lost? I remember that God spoke to me from Gen. 41v32; unto Pharaoh the dream was 'doubled' because 'the thing is established by God, and God will shortly bring it to pass'. I did not know when, but thought it would be soon. God would somehow show me. Because of this growing conviction I declined the offer of a promotion to manage a department in Huston's

Menswear, a few doors further along from Glasgow's in High Street, Newtownards. I explained that to accept would mean a commitment of at least two years to learn the business; this I could not guarantee. Mr Huston, who was a fine Christian gentleman understood. Another offer was to come my way, this time from my father's boss, Mr James Gillies, who wished me to work alongside my father training to manage his business in Royal Avenue, Belfast. Again I refused. God had spoken twice – he would shortly bring it to pass.

My concern for the lost was that which influenced me most in those days. Later in my ministry I came to a fuller appreciation of the various motives for evangelism which I will now set out. I have taught them to various classes of students and in Church group situations, recently in the module on Mission and Evangelism in the School of Practical Theology, in Emanuel University, Romania.

Excursus: Motives for Evangelism

The main motives for evangelism and mission are as follows:

(1) God himself is the God of mission.
R. B. Kuiper,[1] in chapter one of his book *God Centred Evangelism*, sees the triune God as the God of mission and evangelism. Consider (a) God the father as author of evangelism. He conceived evangelism in eternity and commissioned his son (Eph. 1v9-10; 1 Pet. 1v20). He inspired prophets to foretell Messiah's coming and sacrifices to foreshadow (2 Pet. 1v21). He revealed himself in OT acts and chose Israel to be his witness to the nations. He sent his son to die for sinners and the Spirit to enable the church to bear witness. (b) God the Son as author of evangelism. He became man to accomplish the saving work which the father had commissioned him to do. He died a substitutionary death. He commissioned the church and poured out the gift of the Holy Spirit. (c) God the Spirit as author of evangelism. He enabled the prophets and empowered the church; He calls evangelists and guides them in their ministry. He regenerates.

Here we have a great insight concerning the God with whom we profess to have a relationship. As Dr. James S. Stewart[2] *Thine is the Kingdom*, stated:

Concern for world evangelism is not something tacked on to a man's personal Christianity, which he may take or leave as he chooses; it is rooted indefeasibly in the character of the God who has come to us in Christ Jesus. Thus it can never be the province of a few enthusiasts, a sideline or a speciality of a few who have a bent that way. It is the distinctive mark of being a Christian. To accept Christ is to enlist under a missionary banner.

(2) Obedience to Christ
Each of the gospels record Christ's commission to the Church (Matt. 28v19; Mk. 16v15-16; Lk. 24v 47; John. 20v 21). The task of world-wide evangelism is not restricted to the apostles or one section of the Church but is the responsibility of every believer. Latourette,[3] *The First Five Centuries*, is undoubtedly right when he maintains, 'the chief agents in the expansion of Christianity appear not to have been those who made it a profession ... but men and women who earned their livelihood in some purely secular manner and spoke of their faith to those they met in this natural fashion'. Christians are servants (bondslaves) of Christ. (Rom. 1v1; 1 Cor. 6v19-20). Stott[4] affirms in *Motives and Methods in Evangelism*, 'It is sheer hypocrisy to pay lip service to the Lordship of Jesus if we do not heed his command to evangelise. A dumb Christian is a disobedient Christian'. Obedience is the fruit and proof of love, John 14v15.

(3) A sense of obligation and accountability to God
God has given us the task of evangelism (2 Cor. 5v18; Acts 1v8). Paul saw himself as entrusted with the gospel (I Thess. 2:4). One day we must all give account to God (2 Cor. 5: 10-11; Acts 20: 26-27). We are debtors (Rom. 1v14-16).

(4) Compassion for the Lost
See Jesus' compassion (Matt. 9v36) and Paul's (Rom. 9v1-3; Acts 20v31). Why are we not moved? Perhaps we don't take seriously enough the condition of the unsaved as described in the Scriptures. They are without Christ, without hope (Eph. 2: 12) and without excuse, condemned by the general revelation of God in His creation, and by the voice of their own conscience (Rom. 1v18-20; 2v14-16). Hudson Taylor, 'I would never have thought of going out to China had I not believed that the Chinese were lost and needed Christ'.

(5) Concern for the glory of God
Stott[5] considers this to be 'the strongest evangelistic incentive'. In *Our Guilty Silence*, chapter one, he writes of 'The Evangelical Incentive – The Glory of God'. Paul's mission to the nations is 'for the sake of his name', (Rom. 1v5). Also Gaius is commended for his support of those who went forth, 'for his name sake ... taking nothing to the Gentiles'. (3 John v7). 'Love for his name is not a sentimental attachment either to his personal name 'Jesus' or to his official title 'Christ', or to any of his designations in Scripture ... it is a concern for his honour in the world'. Concern for the glory of God is expressed by Elijah (1 Kings. 19v10), the Psalmist (Ps. 119v136), and evidenced in the actions of Paul (Acts 17v16-17) and Jesus (John 2v13-17).
The incentive of the glory of God is the link between our worship and witness.

(a) Worship involves witness. Worship is worth-ship, an acknowledgement of the worth of Almighty God. As Stott[6] maintains, 'It is impossible to worship God and yet not to care two cents whether anybody else worships Him or not'. Therefore a worship which does not beget evangelism is hypocrisy.

(b) Witness also involves worship. Biblical evangelism never puts a full stop after conversion. Converts are for God! Conversion is but a prelude to worship. Once the convert becomes a worshipper he is driven out again into the world as a witness.

(6) The certain hope of the gospel
Andy Lovell (Irish Baptist missionary in Peru from 1971–1998) wrote in the Irish Baptist magazine about Motives for Mission. He made the following points that without hope any enterprise is doomed to failure from the start. The Church has every hope in the success of its mission to evangelise. We have hope (a) in the Person of our God who is Sovereign and all powerful. (b) In the power of the gospel (Rom. 1v16). (c) In the predestinating purpose of God (Rom. 8v29). The mystery of predestination is not a hindrance to mission as some mistakenly think, but it can be a powerful incentive to perseverance. (d) In the prophetic

plan of God. Revelation 7 pictures a multitude which no man could number before the throne.

But the strongest motivation for me during those early days was compassion for the lost.

Amy Carmichael's Dream
One mighty challenge, was a dream by Amy Carmichael (1867-1951) who was born in Millisle, Northern Ireland. She was a missionary in India who opened an Orphanage and founded the Dohnavur Fellowship in 1910 as a sanctuary for over 1000 young women and girls, temple children, who were subjected to customs that amounted to forced prostitution. Recounting the dream[7] she wrote:

'The tom-toms thumped straight on all night and the darkness shuddered round me like a living, feeling thing. I could not go to sleep, so I lay awake and looked; and I saw, as it seemed, this:

That I stood on a grassy sward, and at my feet a precipice broke sheer down into infinite space. I looked, but saw no bottom; only cloud shapes, black and furiously coiled, and great shadow-shrouded hollows, and unfathomable depths. Back I drew, dizzy at the depth.

Then I saw forms of people moving single file along the grass. They were making for the edge. There was a woman with a baby in her arms and another little child holding on to her dress. She was on the very verge. Then I saw that she was blind. She lifted her foot for the next step ... it trod air. She was over, and the children over with her. Oh, the cry as they went over!

Then I saw more streams of people flowing from all quarters. All were blind, stone blind; all made straight for the precipice edge. There were shrieks, as they suddenly knew themselves falling, and a tossing up of helpless arms, catching, clutching at empty air. But some went over quietly, and fell without a sound.

Then I wondered, with a wonder that was simply agony, why no one stopped them at the edge. I could not. I was glued to the ground, and I could only call; though I strained and tried, only a whisper would come.

Then I saw that along the edge there were sentries set at intervals. But the intervals were too great; there were wide, unguarded gaps between. And over these gaps the people fell in their blindness, quite unwarned; and the green grass seemed blood-red to me, and the gulf yawned like the mouth of hell.

Then I saw, like a little picture of peace, a group of people under some trees with their backs turned toward the gulf. They were making daisy chains. Sometimes when a piercing shriek cut the quiet air and reached them, it disturbed them and they thought it a rather vulgar noise. And if one of their number started up and wanted to go and do something to help, then all the others would pull that one down. 'Why should you get so excited about it? You must wait for a definite call to go! You haven't finished your daisy chain yet. It would be really selfish', they said, 'to leave us to finish the work alone'. There was another group. It was made up of people whose great desire was to get more sentries out; but they found that very few wanted to go, and sometimes there were no sentries set for miles and miles of the edge.

Once a girl stood alone in her place, waving the people back; but her mother and other relations called and reminded her that her furlough was due; she must not break the rules. And being tired and needing a change, she had to go and rest for a while; but no one was sent to guard her gap, and over and over the people fell, like a waterfall of souls.

Once a child caught at a tuft of grass that grew at the very brink of the gulf; it clung convulsively, and it called-but nobody seemed to hear. Then the roots of the grass gave way, and with a cry the child went over, its two little hands still holding tight to the torn-off bunch of grass. And the girl who longed to be back in her gap thought she heard the little one cry, and she sprang up and wanted to go; at which they reproved her, reminding her that no one is necessary anywhere; the gap would be well taken care of, they knew. And then they sang a hymn.

Then through the hymn came another sound like the pain of a million broken hearts wrung out in one full drop, one sob. And a horror of great darkness was upon me, for I knew what it was-the Cry of the Blood.

Then thundered a voice, the voice of the Lord. 'And He said, "What hast thou done, The voice of thy brother's blood crieth unto me from the ground"'.

The tom-toms still beat heavily, the darkness still shuddered and shivered about me; I heard the yells of the devil-dancers and weird, wild shriek of the devil-possessed just outside the gate.

What does it matter, after all? It has gone on for years; it will go on for years. Why make such a fuss about it? God forgive us! God arouse us! Shame us out of our callousness! Shame us out of our sin!'

These words from a heart burdened for lost souls moved me to recognise my indebtedness to do all that I could to stand in the gap somewhere ...

The Work of an Evangelist
By the age of eighteen I was preaching week by week. My nineteen sixty three/sixty four dairy has short entries like 29th December 1963, Carrowdore, 'helped of the Lord'; December 31st People's Hall, 'helped of the Lord'; 5th January 1964, Malcolm Lane Mission Hall, (connected to Albertbridge Congregational Church) where the diary reads, 'Failed! God gave me a message of a sinner sunk in sin, but I made it suit any sinners'. I recall that I had preached on Isaiah 1 and I must not have been as faithful in exposing sin as I had intended. Later when I was twenty one years of age I came to the decision to emphasise first in my preaching that men are lost.

However even at this point in my ministry, it is clear that I had a growing concern for lost souls. The entry for Friday January 10th reads, 'Spoke to old man about his soul. Cried. Cannot trust, believe. Commit suicide?' The next day Saturday reads, 'Spoke to old man again. Hardened, despairing yet knows the gospel better than I'. On Sunday 26th January I preached in Killaughy Mission Hall and the next night in Greyabbey Orange Hall Young People's Meeting. The entry reads, 'Good meeting. Helped of the Lord. But I must learn to speak more slowly. The Lord tells me what is wrong with my preaching. Seeking to please men, seeking to please Mrs X (the local organist). I now renounce this. I hate it, desire freedom from it'. Other preaching entries when I was still eighteen include, Kircubbin CWU Hall; Ballystockart, Comber (four Wednesdays on Christ, Son of God; Servant of God; Saviour of the World, Shepherd of the Sheep); Craigavad; Ballyhalbert Gospel Hall; Loughries Mission Hall; Donaghadee; Francis Street Gospel Hall; City Mission Hall, Shankhill Road. Some of these were shared with Harvey as we preached 'two by two'.

Though I was still eighteen I also began to conduct missions. Three in particular I remember. An old hut at the Cottown outside Newtownards on the road to Donaghadee. The meetings (and additional open airs in the area) were held from Sunday 19th July to Sunday 2nd August, 1964. Three of us were involved, Maxie Gray, Harvey and myself. I remember on one of the Sundays, I was preaching first on Exodus 12, the Passover Lamb. After I began I felt deflated, I had no sense of peace or power. Harvey followed, so there was something for those who had attended. At the end of the service I commented to Henry Wilson (whom God had used earlier at the time of my conversion) as to how it had gone. He smiled and said, 'If you had gone up the way you came down, you would have come down the way you went up!' There needs to be true dependence on the Lord and communion with him if we are to have any unction of the Spirit. The entry in my diary for that day reads 'MR MOORE SPOKE', the capitals reflect my self-reliance, rather than upon God the Holy Spirit. More recently, in lecturing on Evangelistic Preaching in the Irish Baptist College and focusing upon unction in preaching, I found help for the lectures from E.M. Bounds and Martyn Lloyd Jones. While one may find it difficult to describe and define unction there are at least three steps which could help to put us in the way of it. First, the Preparation of the Life. What a man is in himself, his whole experience of God, his closeness and communion with him, his whole prayer life will come through in his preaching. Second, the Preparation of the Day. He will be praying and meditating on what God is putting on his heart. Thirdly, the Preparation of the Moment. As he mounts the pulpit, he will do so in dependence on God, lifting up his heart to God and in communion with him asking him for the enabling power of the Holy Spirit. Having done this he can do no other, leaving it with God to either take him up or lay him aside. Finally we should note that the entry in the 1964 diary for 24th October is also significant – it reveals how God was moving in my heart. It simply states, 'Do the work of an Evangelist'. This is clearly the direction my life was taking and would take. On the opening page of my 1965 diary it reads 'Spoke 66 times before this (last year)'. God was fulfilling the truth of Proverbs 18v16, 'a man's gift maketh room for him and bringeth him before great men' – without his trying.

    The second season of blessing took place in a Cottage Mission I shared with Harvey from 3rd – 31st October in the home of Mrs Askin, Dunover

Corner, Ballywalter. It was amazing to see the numbers overflowing the little room and to see God at work. My diary records the themes preached: 'Man Fallen', Genesis 3; 'Lamb of God', John 1v29; 'How Shall we Escape?' Heb.2; 'Great White Throne', 'Serpent of Brass', 'Luke 16 Hell' and other gospel passages. But the more important entries are found in a number of places throughout the weeks, 'woman saved'; 'Mr X from Cardy, saved'; 'Mrs G's little girl saved'; ' X Stewart saved'. This is what makes it all worthwhile. The words of Paul in 1Thess 2v19-20 challenged me continually, 'What is our hope, or joy, or crown of rejoicing. Are not even ye in the presence of our Lord Jesus Christ at his coming? For ye are our joy and crown'. The words of the hymn would move me again and again, 'How many are the lost that I have lifted? How many are the chained I've helped to free? I wonder have I done my best for Jesus? The one who did so much for me'.

The final notable mission was in Ballywalter Gospel Hall with a godly and faithful friend of earlier days, Noel Lowden who was from Downshire Gospel Hall, Holywood. I can still recall the evening a young couple concerned about eternity waited behind to seek for help. Noel took them to the story of the Passover in Exodus 12, when the first-born throughout all Egypt was to die. He painted the picture of two young men in adjoining houses on that fateful night. One young man was pacing up and down visibly moved. He is asked, 'But do you not have the blood on the door? Has not God promised "When I see the blood, I will pass over you?" He responds, 'Yes, I know. But I will not sleep tonight'. Entering the second house we find another young man sitting quietly. 'Is this not the night for the death of the first-born?' He replies 'Yes it is. But did you not see the blood?' Noel came to the punch line. He asked them about these young men. 'Tell me which of these two is the safest?' Of course the point was that they BOTH were safe for BOTH had believed the message and BOTH had the blood sprinkled on the door. The young couple had responded to the good news and turned to Christ; now they were learning that God's promise is sure 'I will pass over you!'

My contacts with Templemore Hall, Belfast, were also memorable experiences for me. As a boy I first went there with Bobby McClements to the Easter Conventions held jointly with The Iron Hall. Bobby did not attend the Grosvenor Hall in Belfast at Easter, where all the assemblies met together. Looking back I now see that this reflects the distance between them and the Ballyhalbert Hall. On many occasions Dr. Tocher, Pastor from the hall, preached in Ballyhalbert; also on Saturday evenings the Templemore Hall Male Voice Choir would come to minister, with their conductor and soloist Joe Nabney. I was also invited to preach on Sundays in Templemore (first recorded dates are March 21st and June 20th 1965) to a full hall or at the Monday Evening Bible Class. I remember those Monday nights in the Tocher Memorial Hall (the minor hall) especially a series on the tabernacle for about 10 weeks or so. Precious times! But I still had a lot to learn. I recall one Sunday morning I used as an illustration the fact that King Edward gave up his throne for Mrs Wallace and made the comparison with our Lord Jesus who in love gave up everything for the church, his bride. Mr Francey, one of the godly elders took me aside and while first thanking me for the blessing he had received through the message, gently but with positive intent pointed out that to use such an illustration was inappropriate and unworthy of our wonderful Lord and his unspeakable sacrifice. The young nineteen year old never used it again.

During this time I met Bob Cousins with whom I was to form a special relationship. He was involved with Ken Brown, Jim Dickson, Billy Houston, Billy Gray and Stanley Rollins in planting a new work situated at Kocknagoney on the outskirts of Belfast. A new hall was to replace the old house where they met. I first preached in the old house on September 19th 1965; special times of blessing lay ahead in future links with Knocknagoney. Bob also brought me to the Ballyvae Orange Hall Annual Conference, near Kilkeel where I had opportunity to preach with some 'Pillars' of the faith, Pastor James Irvine, Newcastle Baptist Church, Dr Paisley and brother Ken Brown from Knocknagoney. I remember Pastor James Irvine, commenting on the fact that he was almost at the point where he was laying down the Lord's armour while I was just putting it on. That is how I saw things myself. I so desired to put on the whole armour of the Lord and to 'stand', Eph. 6v13. Bobby McClements, the 'wee pastor' (as he was affectionately called), by his yearly attendance at the Easter Meetings in Templemore Hall, rather than the Grosvenor Hall, was even at that early stage leading me along a path that would influence my whole future in ministry. I am so grateful for the teaching and fellowship I received from men like him in my formative years and early ministry. I was discovering that God had a wider family than many of those who will call themselves 'separated unto the Lord's name' were prepared to recognise. My course was being planned for the future. During those early years my gift was being used and allowed to develop in the many opportunities afforded both in People's Hall, Portavogie, Kircubbin CWU, Killaughy Mission Hall and elsewhere, not just in the assemblies.

A bond of friendship was formed with another young man, Liam Bell from Rubane. He was employed by Jim Warnock, who had a sizeable farm near his home ... The former altar boy was encouraged by his Christian boss to start reading the Bible again. He was brought into a vital, personal relationship with Christ as he read and responded to John 1v12 'As many as received him to them gave he power to become the sons of God'. He had not attended any local church in the immediate area when he was converted – he went some distance where he would not be known. But then I remember the first Thursday night he walked into the hall in Ballyhalbert. In the providence of God, the local vet, Walter McFerran was preaching that evening on Eph. 2 – being 'spiritually dead' but in the mercy of God coming to new life by grace, not works, through faith in Christ. Here he was also to find his spiritual home. We shared different meetings where he testified how God had revealed to him the possibility of knowing the Lord in a personal way and we often preached together in the open air in the lower Ards. He came to occupy a major role in the leadership team in the hall when Bobby went home to be with the Lord.

'From This Day...' Haggai 2v19
Great! Lunch Hour! This was my time in the secret place with God where I was able to go up into the stock-room on the fourth floor in Glasgow's to read and pray, and then to hurriedly eat lunch. I vividly recall one particular day when my heart filled with the desire to be free to go out to seek the lost as I was reading from the Book of Haggai. I first read from Haggai 1v1-15. On the first day of the sixth month Haggai the prophet had challenged the people who had stopped building the temple BUT STILL were building their own

houses … God had touched their harvests. Haggai exhorted them, 'consider your ways'. In Haggai 2v15-19 I discovered that when they repented and everything really began to move forward, God announced his purpose to bless them. 'Consider now from this day and upward, from the four and twentieth day of the ninth month, even from the day that the foundation of the Lord's temple was laid, consider it. Is the seed yet in the barn? yea, as yet the vine, and the fig tree, and the pomegranate, and the olive tree, hath not brought forth: from this day I will bless you'. I opened my diary and saw that the 24th day of the ninth month was a Saturday in September. Now of course I knew the Jewish calendar would be different but thought it rather significant the 24th was a Saturday – as a Saturday was part of my working week, if I ever gave in my notice I would be leaving at the end of a week. I reflected upon this over and over as I was turning again to Haggai 1v12-15 when God was stirring up the hearts of Zerubbabel and Joshua with the people to begin this great work. It was 'on the twenty-fourth day of the sixth month'. I opened my diary again to realise that it was the very day I was reading the text – 24th June! It was so amazing to be reading it that very day! This was what I needed to bring me to the point of decision. I prayerfully resolved to go to see the boss Mr. Eric in the next few days to specifically inform him that I would be going – not a day before; not a day after the 24th September.

I was advised to seek commendation from a few assemblies, Ballyhalbert, Ballywalter, Holborn Hall, Bangor and Scrabo Hall, Newtownards and this was duly announced in the Witness magazine. I often had opportunity to preach with my friend, Harvey Shaw in these halls. Another hall was the People's Hall, Portavogie where I had preached a number of times. The hall was organised by my good friends Hugh and Jennie Thompson and Hugh Coffey, who attended Ballyhalbert Gospel Hall on Sunday mornings. Once I was convinced of the date of my leaving Glasgow's I went to see Hugh and Jennie informing them not just of my leading to go out to preach, looking to the Lord alone for support, but to begin my Gospel work in People's Hall. After prayerfully considering this for one week, the two Hughs agreed and so as I left my secular employment on the 24th Sept. I began my full-time gospel ministry on the 25th in the evening with a previously arranged opportunity in Aughrim Gospel Hall, South Derry (God was ahead of me in his planning here, as you will see as the story unfolds) and began the Portavogie mission on Sunday 2nd October 1966.

Excursus: Preaching – Content and Manner

In those days as I contemplated a lifetime of preaching which lay before me, in the will of God, it was important to consider how I would preach and what would be the content of my message. Two significant preachers in those days who were mightily used by God, were Pastor Willie Mullan and Dr. Ian Paisley. I determined to adopt their style of preaching, and they became my role models in the gospel. In addition, I also took note of the sermons of Rev. William J. Patton[8] of Dromara, Co. Down edited by Rev. John McIlveen D.D., and recorded in the book *Pardon and Assurance*. William John Patton from Donaghadee became the minister of Second Dromara Presbyterian, ordained there on 29th June 1853 and was a great soul winner with his ministry continuing for forty-one years until his death in 31st January in 1895. Among the sermons recorded in the book are three which are examples of his faithfulness in preaching to lost souls: 'Sin – What it is' 'The Sinfulness of Sin' 'The Wages of Sin'. What impressed me was his faithfulness in exposing sin in the lives and hearts of his people. In his sermon on 'The Sinfulness of Sin' he challenged his people to look at their sin as it is in the light of God's countenance. The main points of the sermon were as follows:

1. *Look at sin in the light of God's holiness*
2. *Look at sin in the light of God's judgements on it upon earth*
3. *Look at sin in the light of a place of eternal punishment*
4. *Look at sin in the light of Christ's death as an atonement for sin*
5. *Look at sin in the light of God's goodness and love to you*

His sermon on The Wages of Sin' also was powerful. He began by saying, 'Let us look into the elements of the curse under which you lie if you have not got Christ as your Saviour, even though you may be amiable, and kind, and moral'.

Then the main points:

1. *You are condemned*
2. *The wrath of God abideth upon you, and you have no God to go to in your*

perplexities and sorrows
3   You are a child of the devil and his slave
4   God may give you up at any time, and cease to strive with you by His Spirit, and may let you alone
5   You may die without Christ
6   You may stand at the judgement-seat without Christ
7   You may suffer everlasting punishment

In preaching all his sermons and making the points outlined above, he used the most explicit language, quoting again and again the warning texts of Scripture. His language could not have been plainer. In the latter sermon[9] he can cry out in his concern for his people, 'No hope – for ever, and for ever, and again for ever! Oh eternity! Eternity! Have you ever thought of being in hell throughout eternity?'

At that time I realised that as far as one's manner in the act of preaching was concerned there was need for a particular approach. Twenty years later in the 1980's I was given opportunity to lecture in the Irish Baptist College on 'Evangelistic Preaching'. I include some principles from the lectures which generally sum up my thinking back when I was beginning to preach. In 1965-66 these were the elements I considered important – in fact vital. They were already in 'seed form' in my mind and I had seen them demonstrated in the powerful preaching of the three men I have just mentioned.

(1) A sense of authority. The preacher should never be apologetic or simply be putting forward some suggestions or ideas. He comes as a sent messenger with a message from God.

(2) A need for freedom. Preaching involves direct contact between the people and the preacher. It is not about reading a manuscript or full notes which will take away from the interplay of personalities. I could take notes into the pulpit, but must not be tied to them. The style might not be as perfect but it makes it possible to leave to the moment the expression of God's truth in Spirit given words.

(3) A sense of concern. Lloyd Jones[10] in *Preaching and Preachers* quoted Richard Cecil, an Anglican preacher of the late 18th century when he wrote, 'To love to preach in one thing, to love those to whom we preach

is quite another'. If the preacher lacks this element of compassion for the people he will also lack the pathos which is a very vital element in all true preaching. Jesus was 'filled with compassion'. Al Martin[11] could insist, 'We must have such a love that will drive us to a sense of responsibility to do all within our power to make the truth of God live to them…What hinders us from being faithful to men is really a form of self-love. We love our own feelings so much that we are afraid to run the risk of offending people and getting them mad at us. Oh they may perish in hell, but that is all right just as long as they perish loving us'.

(4) Sincerity or earnestness in preaching. I remembered that Jesus wept over Jerusalem (Matt. 3v37; Lk. 19v41-42) and with Paul, preaching and weeping went hand in hand (Acts 20v31). Richard Baxter[12] could write: 'How few ministers do preach with all their might? … Alas, we speak so drowsily or gently, that sleeping sinners cannot hear. The blow falls so light that hard hearted persons cannot feel it … What excellent doctrines some ministers have in hand, and let it die in their hands for want of close and lively application … O Sirs, how plainly, how closely and earnestly should we deliver a message of such nature as ours is, when the everlasting life or death of men is concerned in it … Such a work as preaching for men's salvation should be done with all our might – that the people can feel us preach when they hear us'. People will know the seriousness of the gospel and their situation by the seriousness with which we preach to them.

(5) Fire and feeling. We will never move others if we are moved by something ourselves. Examining history, the great preachers of the past, who influenced many, were men of the mighty heart. Lloyd Jones[13] could write, 'The apostle Paul breaks some of the rules of grammar, he interrupts his own argument. It is because of the fire!'

(6) Urgency. I remember being challenged by the story of D. L. Moody the American evangelist, who founded the Moody Church, Chicago. He recounted what he considered to be his greatest mistake on the 8th October 1871, a mistake he determined never to repeat. He had been preaching in the city and that particular night the largest congregation ever was present. He was preaching on Pilate's text, 'What shall I do then

with Jesus which is called Christ?' By the end of the service Moody was very tired. He concluded his message, announced that he would give the audience a week to think over what he had preached. Then they would respond. As a soloist sang the music was drowned out by clanging bells and wailing sirens screaming through the streets. The great Chicago fire was blazing. In the aftermath, hundreds were dead and over a hundred thousand were homeless. Without a doubt, some who heard Moody's message had died in the fire. He reflected remorsefully that he would never give another congregation a week to think over the message of the Gospel. There was need for an urgent response.

I saw this in the preaching of the men mentioned above. They preached for a verdict. People were challenged to do something when the message was over. Lloyd Jones reminded his readers that the one who preaches is not simply imparting information. He is dealing with souls, pilgrims on the way to eternity. In preaching we are involved not only with matters of life and death but with eternal destiny. No-one knows whether we will be alive in a week's time, even a day's time. 'If the preacher does not suggest this sense of urgency, that he is there between God and men, speaking between God and eternity he had no business to be in a pulpit'.[14]

(7) Persuasiveness. In 2 Cor. 5v11, 20 Paul writes, 'Knowing the terror of the Lord we persuade men' and 'we implore you on Christ's behalf, be reconciled to God'. We must not just say things with a 'take it or leave it' attitude. The whole object in preaching is to persuade people. We are not just giving a display of our own knowledge.

(8) The need for direct preaching. Lloyd-Jones[15] explained that sometimes preachers preach *about the* gospel, praising it, saying wonderful things about it. Or preaching it *academically*, analysing it, showing its parts and portions. 'Whereas we are called to preach the gospel to bring it directly to the individuals listening to us and to the whole man'. There must be direct application to the hearers. The individual must be made to understand 'this is for me'.

(9) Plain preaching. Wesley in his first volume of sermons (1746) in the preface emphasised:

> I design plain truths for plain people; therefore of set purpose I abstain from all nice and philosophical speculations, from all perplexed and intricate reasoning; and as far as possible, even from the show of learning unless in sometimes citing the original scripture. I labour to avoid all words which are not easy to understand, all which are not used in common life; and in particular those kinds of technical terms that so frequently occur in bodies of Divinity; those modes of speaking which men of reading are intimately acquainted with but which to the common people are an unknown tongue.

I also had to learn to avoid outworn phrases which would not be understood e.g., 'read your titles clear to mansions in the sky'. Again, it is vital that theological terms should not be given up but rather need to be explained and illustrated. On one occasion in dealing with the Lord's commission to Peter 'Feed my sheep', Spurgeon commented that some preachers seem to have read the text 'Feed my giraffes' because they put the food so high that the sheep cannot reach it. He spoke of the comments of children as a good test of clarity. 'I shall feel I am very faulty in my style if children cannot understand much that I teach in the congregation'.[16] So I needed to remember that a sermon which is not clear would be an indictment against the preacher. I realised the need for short, clear, intelligible statements.

There is no doubt that I attempted to adopt many of these elements of style in my gospel preaching. But style is not all that is important – content is even more vital. It was here that I learned from the two great preachers I mentioned earlier – and from W. J. Patton.

In reflecting upon their preaching I realised that beneath all the preaching lay three main themes – whatever the text or passage i.e., MAN'S RUIN; GOD'S REMEDY; YOUR RESPONSIBILITY.

Man's ruin involves showing to men that they are condemned sinners. My thinking has remained the same for 50 years and is expressed in my recent book on 1&2 Timothy and Titus[17]:

> If we have been like Paul 'appointed a preacher' (1 Tim. 2v7), we ought to recognise the importance of getting people first of all to the place where they realise that they are condemned sinners. What is the point of calling on our hearers to 'come to Jesus' if they have no clear idea why they have to come? They need to be made to see that they are sinners

condemned, under the wrath of God, and without hope, apart from the salvation proclaimed in the gospel. How can we make them aware of the fact that they are lost and condemned? Of course one answer is to preach the 10 commandments, to challenge their consciences as to the many, many ways they have transgressed – to use the law as Paul is advocating here. It is those who realise their sin who will flee to the saviour, 'the one mediator between God and man'. Often in preaching I have tried – in love – to stress, 'You will NEVER BE in heaven until first of all you realise that you ARE NOT going there!' Such an emphasis is clearly missing from much preaching today. The wonderful news is that when we could do nothing to change this – no works (Tit. 3v5; 2 Tim. 1v9); no payment (1 Pet. 1v18; Acts 8v18-21), God in grace (which is NOT just unmerited favour, but favour AGAINST merit – when we deserve the opposite, God's wrath) took the initiative in sending his son as the ransom (1Tim. 1v15; 2v5-6; 2 Tim. 1v9-10; Tit. 2v11-14).

Here we are discovering the answer to our need – God's answer in the cross work of Christ. I knew the importance of preaching the remedy announcing to sinners that all that needs to be done has been done by Christ at the cross. People have the responsibility to believe the good news, repent of their rebellion and submit themselves to him.

So I came more and more to see what and how I was to preach the gospel. Later when lecturing on Evangelistic Preaching in the College I discovered a discussion by Packer[18] which concisely summed up what I attempted to do. He writes about evangelistic preaching:

> Evangelistic preachers and personal workers have sometimes been known to make this mistake. In their concern to focus attention on the atoning death of Christ, as the sole sufficient ground on which sinners may be accepted with God, they have expounded the summons to saving faith in these terms: 'Believe that Christ died for your sins'. The effect of this exposition is to represent the saving work of Christ in the past, dissociated from His Person in the present, as the whole object of our trust. But it is not biblical thus to isolate the work from the Worker. Nowhere in the New Testament is the call to believe expressed in such terms. What the New Testament calls for is faith in *(en)* or into *(eis)* or upon *(ein)* Christ Himself, the placing of our trust in the living Saviour, who died for sins. The object of saving faith is thus not, strictly speaking, the atonement, but the Lord Jesus Christ, who made atonement. We must not in presenting the gospel isolate the cross and its benefits from the Christ whose cross it was. For the

persons to whom the benefits of Christ's death belong are just those who trust His Person, and believe, not upon His saving death simply, but upon *Him*, the living Saviour. 'Believe on *the Lord Jesus Christ*, and thou shalt be saved', said Paul. 'Come unto *me* and I will give you rest', said our Lord.

This being so, one thing becomes clear straight away: namely, that the question about the extent of the atonement, which is being much agitated in some quarters, has no bearing on the content of the evangelistic message at this particular point. I do not propose to discuss this question now; I have done that elsewhere. I am not at present asking you whether you think it is true to say that Christ died in order to save every single human being, past, present, and future, or not. Nor am I at present inviting you to make up your mind on this question, if you have not done so already. All I want to say here is that even if you think the above assertion is true, your presentation of Christ in evangelism ought not to differ from that of the man who thinks it false. What I mean is this. It is obvious that if a preacher thought that the statement, 'Christ died for every one of you', made to any congregation, would be unverifiable, and probably not true, he would take care not to make it in his gospel preaching. You do not find such statements in the sermons of, for instance, George Whitefield or Charles Spurgeon. But now, my point is that, even if a man thinks that this statement would be true if he made it, it is not a thing that he ever needs to say, or ever has reason to say, when preaching the gospel. For preaching the gospel, as we have just seen, means inviting sinners to come to Jesus Christ, the living Saviour, who, by virtue of His atoning death, is able to forgive and save all those who put their trust in Him. What has to be said about the cross when preaching the gospel is simply that Christ's death is the ground on which Christ's forgiveness is given. And this is all that has to be said. The question of the designed extent of the atonement does not come into the story at all.

The fact is that the New Testament never calls on any man to repent on the ground that Christ died specifically and particularly for him. The basis on which the New Testament invites sinners to put faith in Christ is simply that they need Him, and that He offers Himself to them, and that those who receive Him are promised all the benefits that His death secured for His people. What is universal and all-inclusive in the New Testament is the invitation to faith, and the promise of salvation to all who believe.

Our task in evangelism is to reproduce as faithfully as possible the New Testament emphasis. To go beyond the New Testament, or to distort its viewpoint or shift its stress, is always wrong. And therefore if we may at this point speak in the words of James Denney 'we do not think of separating (Christ's) work from Him who achieved it'. The New Testament knows only of a living Christ, and all apostolic preaching of the gospel holds up the living Christ to men. But the living Christ is Christ who died, and He is never preached apart from His death, and from its reconciling power. It is *the living Christ, with the virtue of His reconciling death in Him,* who is the burden of the apostolic message. The task of the evangelist is to preach *Christ in His character as the Crucified.* The gospel is not, believe that Christ died for everybody's sins, and therefore for yours, any more than it is, believe that Christ died only for certain people's sins, and so perhaps not for yours. The gospel is, believe on the Lord Jesus Christ, who died for sins, and now offers you Himself as your Saviour. This is the message which we are to take to the world. We have no business to ask them to put faith in any view of the extent of the atonement; our job is to point them to the living Christ, and summon them to trust in Him.

It was because they had both grasped this that John Wesley and George Whitefield could regard each other as brothers in evangelism, though they differed on the extent of the atonement. For their views on this subject did not enter into their gospel preaching. Both were content to preach the gospel just as it stands in Scripture: that is, to proclaim 'the living Christ, with the virtue of His reconciling death in Him', to offer Him to sinners, and to invite the lost to come to Him and so find life.

So basic content was clear – man's ruin, God's remedy, your responsibility. But still while the preaching was clear I had so much still to learn about how to handle a text or a passage, how to 'rightly divide' the word of God. This will be our focus later in my story.

People's Hall, Portavogie

The first mission was a demanding but truly blessed time. I preached for the whole five weeks to a full hall. God moved in many hearts by his Spirit. I recall especially some young teenage girls who attended night after night. All five came to know the Lord and went on to prove the reality of God's work within them. Also an old fisherman of over 90 years of age – Mr K – who lived just round the corner from the hall, in the terrace row facing the harbour. God was merciful to him at this time of life and saved him. In the following year, as happens when you are older, he was not sleeping well one particular night. He walked out of his little terrace house and unto the harbour, to reminisce about old times but fell into the water and was drowned. Yet it would have been 'absent from the body, present with the Lord' (2 Cor. 5v8). I had preached a lot in many halls in the Ards Peninsula and now here were another five weeks! I needed to be fresh with new texts to share in preaching the gospel. As one night finished I had to seek God for what I would preach the next night. One evening as we travelled back by car with the 'wee pastor' Bobby McClements he suggested the following theme. Job 40v4, 'Behold I am vile' – a text that TAKES OUR PRIDE AWAY; John 1v29, 'Behold the Lamb of God' – a text that TAKES OUR SIN AWAY; Rev. 3v20 – a text that TAKES OUR DOUBT AWAY; Rev. 22v12, 'Behold I come Quickly' – a text the TAKES YOURSELF AWAY. A few nights later I used the outline he had suggested. His only comment as we shook hands on the way out was, 'Borrowed tools sometimes work well!' Other missions followed in places like Killaughy Mission Hall (January '67); Calhame Orange Hall, Cloughey (Feb. '67) with a friend at the time, Bert Johnstone. Then our coasts expanded again and we were back in Belfast.

Knocknagoney Mission
Earlier I have referred to my first visit to Knocknagoney in 1965. I had preached in the old hall and walked the site for the new building with the late Bob Cousins. What a man of vision! He had explained how God had directed him to lay the foundation on the edge of the needy Knocknagoney Estate. The work was being blessed and a Sunday School was going well. Christians from other churches in Belfast came to teach, including a girl from the Ravenhill Road Free Presbyterian Church, called Eileen Owens – a young lady unknown to me. Dr. Paisley was supportive of Bob Cousins – as of course was Templemore Hall, where Bob attended. It was good to be involved in this church plant.

Now I was out in faith as an Evangelist and the invitation came to have a mission from 5th – 31st March. Two things stand out in my memory of those weeks. First, the days with Billy Houston (father of the present pastor of Mountpottinger Baptist), as we walked the streets of the estate talking to the residents about why the mission was being held. Second, my 'Belfast taxi' service duties each night. Among those who came out from Belfast to support the mission was Mrs Kathleen Scott, 74 Tildarg Street and the Sunday School teacher, Eileen Owens. Mrs Scott faithfully knitted hats for Walter Burrell who served with the Seamen's Christian Friends Society in Cork. She also had a great regard for Bobby Cousins and his burden for Knocknagoney.

Eileen had been approached by Bob to play each evening during the Gospel outreach. She agreed and duly arrived the first night, by her own admission 'to play for some old boy who was having a mission'.

Bob asked if I would deliver the two ladies back to Belfast after the meetings and as I was staying during the three weeks of mission with my Aunt Peggy in Florida Drive I readily agreed to assist. All was organised. First stop Tildarg Street, the home of Mrs. Scott, continuing on to Cherryville Street, where Eileen lived. Final destination, parking outside the home of my Aunt. Mrs Scott, (mother of Wesley Scott, later to become a valued friend and co-worker with me during my years as pastor of Castlereagh Baptist) stated that she was greatly blessed during the mission. She claimed her prayer life was deepened, although I was told that part of the reason for this was the speed of the drive from Knocknagoney to Tildarg Street. Cherryville Street was to become a regular parking place for me over the next months. I have outlined earlier that ever since God stopped me on my wayward path with the car crash in 1962 I had been radical in my focus. Work, study of the word, work again was the pattern. This was how I had lived my life for the past four years. Now that was about to change as I realised that God had brought Eileen Owens into my life to share it and support me for 39 years.

It was not long until Eileen felt the same guidance about our relationship. It was important for both of us to sense the leading of the Lord. Eileen had been hurt in a former relationship making her hesitant about commitment. But she told me that God spoke to her through a passage in 2 Cor. 2v8-9. The word seemed so direct, about 'confirming your love toward him' and stating: 'For to this end also did I write, that I might know the proof of you, whether ye be obedient in all things'. God had given us a love for each other. She often recalled that early in our relationship after we met I asked, 'Can you type?' She was to be such help in years to come, typing my 20,000 word MTh thesis on a little typewriter and then even more demanding my PhD on an Amstrad! This demonstrates a little of her love and total commitment to me and to the Lord.

South Derry

My first visit to the area was on Sunday 25th September 1966. The late Hedley Murphy, the radio evangelist, also associated with the Assemblies recommended me to come. I just had stepped out into full-time work and on that first Sunday evening preached in Aughrim Gospel Hall. Robert Willie Davis was one of the leading brethren in the hall working with others like James Corbett and Bertie Pickering. After the meeting he just extended to me the opportunity to come to conduct Gospel meetings if ever I felt led – as the assemblies do. He suggested after Easter the following year. So the door was open. The mission in Knocknagoney continued right up until the Friday of Easter week and I headed for South Derry on the Sunday to start again. I had called to see Bertie Pickering in the earlier part of Easter week as he attended the yearly Assemblies meeting in Grosveror Hall. He seemed a little unclear about when we would start as there was another Gospel mission on in the Hospital Road Assembly, Magherafelt but said to come ahead anyway and we would discuss things when I arrived.

That first Sunday after Easter in Aughrim was a 'typical' Sunday for me in those days. My diary states that the day began in the Sunday School in Aughrim at 11.00 am as I spoke to the children; 12.00 in the Morning meeting (my Free Presbyterian girlfriend Eileen sitting in the back seat) I spoke on Hebrews 4, our Great High Priest; 6.00 pm in the Gospel Meeting on Eph. 2 and finally, in the Youth Fellowship in the Presbyterian Church, Antrim at 8.15pm on the four 'therefores' of Romans. It was decided by the brethren in the hall that the rest of the week would be devoted to pray for the mission – also to allow the other mission in Magherafelt to finish. It was an encouragement when the friends from the Knocknagoney mission came all the way from Belfast on one of those prayer evenings to show their support.

The time in Aughrim Gospel Hall was a special season of blessing. I stayed for a few weeks in the home of the late Samuel Scott, then moved to 'the Prophet's Chamber' as it was called, a little extension built on to the traditional farmhouse of Mr and Mrs James Corbett situated close to the hall. Here Mrs Corbett cared for me in love for the Lord. There were many opportunities to visit in the area and down into Castledawson. Hearing reports of my daily calls, James would often comment that once or twice I had been 'in the lion's den' and he did not mean the unconverted! There was a lot of spiritual pressure involved in such an intense programme. I was just twenty one years of age, away from home and constantly labouring alone. One day as I was finding it particularly difficult, brother Bob Cousins was passing with his lorry and stopped in Magherafelt to assure me again of the prayer support of the Knocknagoney people. I remember how we kneeled in the back of the lorry and prayed together that God in his grace would strengthen me – a precious moment I have never forgotten.

The mission continued for over seven weeks. God moved in a remarkable way with news of conversions reported week by week. One I particularly remember was brother Uel Finlay. Uel was a young trainee in Feldon House, Belfast. He was persuaded to come to the Sunday evening Gospel meeting and that I would then take him to Belfast to the place where he stayed to be ready for work on Monday. God spoke to him in a powerful way at that time so that one Sunday as we travelled to Belfast after the meeting we pulled in the car by the side of the road and he came to Christ for salvation. I praise God that I have many 'spiritual grandchildren' because of the ministry of brother Uel down through almost fifty years. It was good to return to Aughrim a number of weeks after the mission for a baptismal service. Cold water was brought in creamery cans so that young people like Roland and Ralph Pickering who grew up in the hall could be baptised. I had not baptised before – so I was just as it were thrown in at the deep end! But things were to change for me in South Derry.

Christians from many places around South Derry had attended the original mission. Not long after that I was invited to preach in the Desertmartin Union Hall and was given a number of dates. Some of the young men in Aughrim were anxious for me as to how this would be understood by local brethren assemblies. But I pointed out that I could not be two different men – one in South Derry and another in Belfast. Therefore I took the opportunities I was given outside the assemblies and other invitations followed. The late Ernie Campbell was a good friend and a tent mission was organised at Townparks, Magherafelt commencing in August 1967 for five and a half weeks. It is surely providential that during the mission I was given kind hospitality in the home of Mr and Mrs Tom McClure. Tom was partner in the motor firm Rainey and McClure Motors in Magherafelt, but providentially, was also the Secretary of the Baptist Church in the town. Other opportunities followed in different places – going to Ayr to John

14 Victoria Gardens
13-2-68

My Dear Son

We thank you for the many letters we have received from you since you left; you have kept us very well informed about your doings. Here is a letter that came yesterday; it might need an answer before you get back.

We are looking forward to seeing you again. Hope things are going alright with you. Most people around here are Remembering you where it matters.

With Love from Mum & Dad.

Moore's church as the preacher for the Templemore Hall Male Voice Choir; Diverna Orange Hall, near Bessbrook; a four week mission in Magherascuse in fellowship with Comber Baptist Church; back in Magherafelt to the Christian Workers Union Hall for a Children's Mission and Youth Mission where a number of young people professed conversion. From time to time during these 'mission' weeks I would return to Belfast to see my girlfriend Eileen. Rather than travel on to Ballyhalbert (another twenty-five miles), I would stay in the home of brother Bob and Nancy Cousins from Knocknagoney. I had a key and when they knew I would be coming they would lift little Ina, one of their children, from her bed and leave it for me.

Of particular significance for the future was an invitation to preach for the first time in Magherafelt Baptist Church on Sunday, 14th January, 1968. A further week of meetings on the tabernacle followed in Magargy Orange Hall, near Moneymore. A month of Saturday evenings were spent in Portadown Christian Workers Union with young people. Then it was off to Ramsay, Isle of Man to the Seaman's Christian Bethel (the missionary was Hugh Wilson, brother of Henry, mentioned earlier in the book) where the Mission lasted three and a half weeks. Here I first met Val English and his wife Eileen, who later would come to Northern Ireland to serve the Lord in a variety of ministries, but first in Monkstown Baptist Church. He was pastor of Douglas Baptist Church and brought some young people over to Ramsay to help us in the outreach. We were now into March to another Mission in The Iron Hall Assembly, Belfast.

As you will realise with such an itinerary I was away from home a lot and sometimes when out of Northern Ireland I had to keep in touch with Eileen by letter. Also I was always careful to keep constant contact with my parents. They had made many sacrifices especially when I reached the decision that God was calling me into full-time work. Yet they remained fully supportive as their letters revealed. I was living totally by faith, but God met all my needs, putting it in the hearts of various individuals to help me – even down to my travel.

Magherafelt Baptist Church

Throughout the early months of 1968 the awareness of a growing sense of commitment to South Derry occupied my thoughts. I was invited again to

CALLING ALL YOUNG PEOPLE!

Hear...

MR. HAMILTON MOORE

In Magherafelt C.W.U. Hall, Garden Street, from (D.V.) 4th—13th December inclusive

CHILDREN'S SERVICES at 6 p.m.
Each Evening (Saturdays & Sundays excepted)
CHORUSES — PRIZES — BIBLE STORIES

TEENS & TWENTIES HOUR at 8 p.m.
Each Evening (Sunday excepted)
MUSICAL GROUPS - INFORMAL CHAT - TEA

These are your Meetings
COME YOURSELF AND BRING A FRIEND

"Remember now thy Creator in the days of thy youth"—ECC. 12 v 1.

COLLECTING POINTS—
QUEEN'S AVENUE—Library   BEECHLAND GDNS.—Garages
GLENBURN PARK—Sign.   WESTLAND RD.—Telephone Kiosk
Time of Collection 5.45 p.m.
Parents—There will be supervision at all of these points

preach for a full week in Magherafelt Baptist Church on various biblical themes. It became more and more clear that God was placing this area on my heart. When the Office Bearers met with me at the end of the week, I shared with them my sense of leading, resulting in a unanimous call to the Church. God had been exercising my mind through verses where Paul evangelised in Corinth and felt compelled of the Spirit and clearly directed of the Lord to remain for a longer period. Acts 18v8-11 records, 'And Crispus, the chief ruler of the synagogue, believed on the Lord with all his house; and many of the Corinthians hearing believed, and were baptised. Then spake the Lord to Paul in the night by a vision, Be not afraid, but speak, and hold not thy peace: For I am with thee, and no man shall set on thee to hurt thee: for I have much people in this city. And he continued there a year and six months, teaching the word of God among them'. God had worked in my ministry in the whole South Derry area. Even in that week in the Baptist Church, different family members of people who had been associated with the Church came to know the Lord. It was confirmation of the direction the Spirit was leading.

(B) Hamilton Moore – Pastor

The Induction Service was organised for the 3rd July 1968 in the Magherafelt CWU Hall. Bobby McClements did not come; I expect for a couple of reasons – the distance, the awkwardness of the situation. But Liam Bell did come and spoke on my behalf. Pastor Hugh Orr and Pastor Boggs were there to deliver the charge, one to the Church and the other to me. I remember particularly the word brought by Pastor Boggs of Tobermore and Carndaisy Baptist Churches. He preached on Exodus 17v8-16, the action of Aaron and Hur in v12 when the arms of Moses became weary. 'But Moses' hands were heavy; and they took a stone, and put it under him, and he sat thereon; and Aaron and Hur stayed up his hands, the one on the one side and the other on the other side; and his hands were steady until the going down of the sun'. He had a unique skill in sermon presentation. The text was really the statement 'they took a stone and put it under him'. He explained that they did not throw stones at him but engaged in a ministry of support. He had three points of exhortation for the church regarding their new pastor. GIVE HIM YOUR

HEAD – be present under the preaching of the word, to learn and grow in your knowledge of the Lord. GIVE HIM YOUR HEART – remembering him in prayer and showing him that you respect and accept him. Finally, GIVE HIM YOUR HAND – supporting him in every way possible. This message is so relevant and important in many church situations today.

54 Moneymore Road
So began my ministry in Magherafelt for the next six years. However I was not to face it alone. From July to September I was single and enjoying the hospitality of Granny Dale in her bungalow in Highfield Road (and her singing of the old gospel hymns from early morning). But my relationship from March 1967 with Eileen had matured. We were engaged around Christmas and married on Monday, September 16th, 1968 in the Old Ravenhill Free Presbyterian Church with Dr Paisley presiding. A rather humorous incident happened the previous day. After preaching in Magherafelt Baptist in the evening before my marriage I stopped on the way back to Ballyhalbert in Castledawson Memorial Hall, where brother Tommy Loughrey held a Gospel Meeting. I chose to preach on Revelation 20, the Great Judgment Day. One can never forget the solemnity of the subject and although we treated it with the necessary seriousness, one or two in the congregation could not help but smile when the theme was first announced.

But it was no judgment day for me, rather the day I had looked forward to for a long time. Eileen and I resided at 54 Moneymore Road where we served the Lord together. It is important to understand the great opportunities which were available to us in those days. Our marriage was mid September, but my diary was filled with commitments through October – 36 in total as I preached in Magherafelt, in Castledawson, Cookstown and conducted a mission in Knockbracken Mission hall, Carryduff at the same time. My wife was a rock of total support, making it possible for me to carry out such a full programme. This schedule was typical of those days with many more missions and meetings conducted in the South Derry area, different parts of Northern Ireland and elsewhere e.g., Bellaghy, Tobermore, Ballyronan, Ballymaguigan, Carndaisy, Rathcoole, Tullynure, Groggan Old School, Tintagh, Lisnagleer, Armagh Baptist Church, Castlereagh Baptist, Carryduff, Lisburn, Scrabo

Hall, Newtownards, Glenarm, Isle of Man, Forth, Scotland. I was privileged to speak on a number of occasions for Evangelical Youth Movement, Director Ed Adams. Groups of young people would go on weekends and often part of my holidays away from Magherafelt in the summer was spent in places like Donegal or Ostend, Belgium for evangelistic outreach. Also Tom McClure's Bible Study for some young men on Wednesday evening in the church became a weekly Bible Class for all ages. Inside two years the new church building on the Ballyronan Road was finished and the work progressed with more people added to the membership.

I recall one couple with their family, the Wilsons who had been in the church not only from the beginning of my ministry, but for many years. B and his wife were totally committed to everything in the fellowship but B was not baptised or in membership. I had often preached on baptism and affirmed first that it was ordained by the Lord himself, not the Baptists or some other grouping and that every Christian in Acts was a baptised believer. We were going to heaven to worship one who was himself a baptised man and whatever was left undone here will be undone for all eternity! B would explain that he thought that an arranged meeting for a baptism would be difficult for him as he was a backward person. He loved the beach at Downhill on the North Antrim Coast and often with family he would go there. He would reveal his thoughts that if only I was down sometime and challenged him, 'What is keeping you from confessing your faith before these people on the beach? Will you be baptised?' then he would confess his faith in this God ordained way. So one afternoon I went to his little house in Golf Terrace and announced to him, 'I am going to Ballyronan, to the Lough Shore. You must come now and be baptised'. What a moment when at the side of the Lough, he went down fully clothed into the water with me, before the people in the car park, the Children's playground, and any other Ballyronan residents nearby and was baptised! He became a faithful member of the church all the time I was there.

The one thing which impressed me during those days was the welcome I received among Baptist people. It may be true that for many particular groups of Christians it is easy to adopt a mentality that we have got it right and to doubt the orthodoxy or even the salvation of all the others. We can find ourselves in a sense brainwashed without even realising it. One recalls the words of the Lord Jesus to his disciples when John reveals his criticism of 'one casting out devils in thy name, and he followeth not us'. John had forbidden him because 'he followeth not us'. Jesus said 'He who is not against us is on our part', (Mk. 9v38-41). I certainly had struggled when faced with making choices about my ministry and the direction it should take. I remember a number of Mondays back in September 1966 when I borrowed a model of the tabernacle from a certain Brethren Evangelist to use in Templemore Hall. He was willing to let me borrow it but it also led to a discussion of my goals in ministry and how I considered God was leading me. I affirmed my desire to preach the gospel and to help the Assemblies. He suggested that he could help me – it was a normal thing for Brethren Evangelists to serve or labour two by two. I could see that he was willing to either take me under his own wing or suggest another Evangelist with whom I could labour. But it became clear that for this to happen I would have to commit myself to preach only among the assemblies separated unto the Lord's name. Already I had experienced some bookings cancelled in certain assemblies because my name had appeared in the Belfast Telegraph preaching in Templemore Hall and NOT in the column reserved only for Assemblies. Soon I was to find myself being preached at from the pulpit (but not named) by a leading English Brethren Evangelist. Pressure was being applied for me to change direction, to refuse to accept certain invitations – I suppose the crisis as I saw it was, would I limit my ministry to please men or continue to have the liberty to choose before God the way ahead. Seeking the advice of a friend the choice was made – to change nothing but just continue as I had been doing for the past few years. This I did! I did not leave the assemblies, they left me – certain ones at least. Yet the contrast to such rejection was the welcome, love and support felt in the Baptist Churches where I had opportunity to minister. At my first Conference meeting with other pastors (actually in the Irish Baptist College, Sandown Road, which was to be my future place of service) I recall the late L.E. Deens of Grosvenor Road Baptist Church, Dublin greeting me with the words, 'Welcome to the ranks!'

For six years I served the Lord in the South Derry area, preaching and teaching in the Baptist Church and in the whole area and wider afield. Eileen helped in the women's work, visiting with me on occasions, at other times visiting alone. A wise counsellor, proving to be a true helpmeet, often restraining my impetuous spirit, advising me to take time, weigh up certain aspects before making choices. When our first child, Wendy Christine Moore was born on 16th October, 1971 in the Mid-Ulster Hospital, our joy was complete.

On The Road Again

I still had a burden to preach the gospel beyond the immediate area. When the call to Magherafelt Baptist Church was sent to me there were no conditions attached. However, the meeting was chaired by Pastor R.A. Boggs of Tobermore and although I was not given any information (rightly so) of what happened on the night, I know from the letter I received he introduced a discussion about the help that the Irish Baptist College might be to me. I was still young (not yet twenty three years of age) with no formal training. So the letter had details of the unanimous call with a final sentence that the church would encourage me to make use of any possible assistance the College could provide for me.

I must confess at the time I was clear about how I should respond to the call to serve God in South Derry. For months God was already at work in my heart burdening me about the needs and opportunities in that area. But the College? That was another matter. My years in the Gospel Hall, Ballyhalbert with the 'brethren' influence and having Pastor Willie Mullan as a 'mentor' learning from his witness and preaching – although I never had the opportunity to attend his Bible Class – meant that I had been content to enrol in 'Mary's Bible School' i.e., sitting at the feet of Jesus. I resolved to accept the call – I could do no other for I knew that God had brought it to pass. As for the encouragement regarding the College, I would consider it for the future but really had little intention of making the connection any time soon. I reckoned that quite a few of the members present that night or even some of the office bearers would probably not be reminding me of that statement in the near future and so it proved. So Pastor Boggs wise foresight was not quickly taken up.

The fact was that after a few years in Magherafelt I began to have a growing sense of 'gaps' in my knowledge that would need to be filled. I had really dropped out of school at 15. When I was moved up a year because of the change in the Examination system from Junior and Senior to GCSE and A Levels, as I have explained earlier, I did not settle well. The easy way out was to leave and start to work. But now my thinking was different. So I decided to commence my education as I had to on the bottom rung of the ladder, enrolling in the London Bible College's Correspondence Courses for 'O' and 'A' Level courses, plus another 'A' Level in Political Studies with Wolsey Hall, Oxford.

These studies were already under way when the time came for me to move on from Magherafelt. I was (and always will be) an evangelist at heart. The ministry I felt called to was to either plant or to 'grow' a small church until it becomes stronger and then to move on to another challenge. So on 23rd May 1974, after six years of preaching and teaching with the full support of my family I was on the road again. We stored our furniture for a few months and moved down to my parents' home in Victoria Gardens, Ballyhalbert. My evangelistic work began immediately within two weeks – in Dromore Baptist Church with Pastor Alan Kerr. Other opportunities followed throughout the following months: Donacloney Orange Hall; Limavady, Larne, Antrim, with the Lord's blessing and on into 1975. Within a short time we were offered accommodation in West Winds Estate, Newtownards which shortened the travel distance to different parts of the Province. The Moore family became members of Newtownards Baptist Church, under the ministry of Pastor Sam Carson.

At this time I was to renew a link with Glenarm. Mr John Morrow, his wife Margaret and family lived in the village where Mrs Morrow had a Café/Guesthouse in Altmore Street. As a family they were first associated with the Non-Subscribing Presbyterian Church, Glenarm, but God had graciously enlightened them and they were now deeply burdened that others might hear the true Gospel and believe. 'Jock' as he was affectionately known had organised meetings in his café on a Sunday afternoon. He was a great witness for the Lord in the village. Since people knew of his stand they were often drawn to his home (some even when they were under the influence) to speak about the things of God. Jock and Margaret's kitchen was the place where many first heard the way of salvation. Through Mrs Morrow's culinary skills, others, especially older people, heard what Christ had done for them when they would attend the special dinners organised at different times of year in the café.

How was I first introduced to the work in Glenarm? I recall leaving Magherafelt one Sunday afternoon for the 4.30 pm service in the café, then jumping in the car around 5.00 pm to be back to preach in Magherafelt at 6.30 pm. Now back in evangelism again, I was able to assist Glenarm more effectively than earlier. From January 1975 I often was involved in what turned out to be a new church plant. My diary from 10th has the entry 'Glenarm Starts'. The reference is to the special Coffee Bar Mission. Some of the present members of Glenarm trace their conversion to this time. One person who was a great help in the mission and subsequently, was a young man called Geoffrey, son of Bobby and Barbara Mills. No one could foresee that he was to be called home as the result of a motor bike accident a few months later in the early hours of 6th June just three days after his 18th birthday. Geoffrey was saved in 1972 and from that moment lived to witness for Christ and was looking forward to going to Bible College. In the booklet edited by his mother Mrs. Barbara Mills[19] there is a brief account of his first coming to Glenarm.

> He felt, although he had been on Outreach work during the spring and summer, that he ought to be doing more for his Lord and Saviour... He was led to a coffee bar mission in the Glenarm Evangelical Centre, the speaker being Mr. Hamilton Moore (evangelist). Geoffrey was keen to help. Now he had found a place where he knew he would be doing something for his Lord. From then his interests all lay in trying to win others for Jesus Christ. Almost every evening found him at Glenarm; if not at a meeting, he was trying to encourage someone to come along. Many profitable meetings were held in Glenarm Evangelical Centre, and many young people can call it their spiritual Birth Place, whereof we give God the Glory – great things He hath done.

The Booklet[20] continues:

> He had a real love for these young folk and the ability to mix with them and very soon became a spiritual leader to many. Not only did he help us in these meetings, but quite often used his car to transport some of his young friends to the mission. This was a great help and encouragement to us... After the mission he continued to be a real witness, especially to the young believers, coming down many evenings to have fellowship with them and to talk to them more about this new life in Christ.

But on the evening of 5th June he borrowed a motor bicycle to take it for a short run. He was not used to it and on the Straidkelly Road, Glenarm, an accident occurred and only the Lord knows what happened. The Glenarm doctor finally arrived and although Geoffrey did not appear to have many injuries, the ambulance from the Larne Hospital was summoned. As he waited he witnessed to all who were gathered around and then as he was being transported to the Larne Hospital. The Sister of the ward feared inward bleeding and, as Geoffrey continued to speak about his Lord, he was taken to the operating theatre where during the administration of anaesthetic he passed into the presence of the King. God brought many young people to Christ as a result of his home call, some even through the funeral services. The following is a transcript of the message I delivered at the Memorial Service.

Excursus: Memorial Service

The substance of the message brought by Pastor Hamilton Moore at Geoffrey's Memorial Service in the Glenarm Evangelical Centre, July 3rd, 1975

Readings (I Thess. 4v13-18; Job 14v10)

The verse I want to take as a basis for my message to you is Job 14v10: 'But man dieth and wasteth away: yea, man giveth up the ghost, and where is he?' Geoffrey Mills – where is he? Where is Geoffrey just now?

I believe we can say first of all that HE IS ABSENT AS FAR AS HIS FAMILY AND FRIENDS ARE CONCERNED. They know he's absent and they feel their great loss. They will need to look to the Lord more and more, for he is the only one who can give them strength to face the days which lie ahead.

In Acts 27 there was a time in the life of the apostle Paul when he was journeying to Rome as a prisoner to stand before Caesar. The little ship in which he was travelling ran into a great storm. It was being blown and battered and many were sure that they were going to perish. In verse 29 we read, 'they cast four anchors out of the stern and wished for the day'. Four anchors to stabilize the ship, four anchors to save them in the midst of the storm. This is only a historical event but it illustrates the point I want to make. There are anchors for Geoffrey's friends and loved ones too which they can lay hold of to help them in these days – *the anchor of the Scriptures*, from which they will derive comfort and strength: *the anchor of the throne of grace*, where they will find grace to help in this time of need: *the anchor of the love of God*, for he does know and care and they can trust him: *the anchor of the blessed hope*, knowing this is not the end but that there is a glorious day of re-union when Jesus comes. 'We shall not prevent (precede) them which are asleep' but shall be 'caught up together'. What a moment that will be! Yes, there are anchors for the soul, anchors to lay hold of and they will support you in the midst of the storm.

But as we think about where Geoffrey is, I believe we can say that he is not only absent with regard to his family and friends but also that HE IS WITH CHRIST WITH REGARD TO HIS SOUL AND SPIRIT. In 2 Cor. 5v8 we read to be 'absent from the body' is to be 'present with the Lord'. There is no soul sleep or unconscious state between death and resurrection. The Christian who dies is 'with Christ which is far better' (Philippians 1v23).

There was a time when Geoffrey Mills was '*without Christ*' as we read in Ephesians 2v12, 'having no hope'. Are you without Christ? You may have many things but if you are without Christ you are without hope. There are many things you can get to heaven without. You can get to Heaven without money, without fame, without power and influence, without houses and lands, but you cannot get to heaven without Christ. Yes, Geoffrey was just like you, without Christ, a sinner, separated from God by sin and facing his judgment, facing hell, but there was a day when he *received Christ* into his life as his personal Saviour and put his trust in his sacrifice for sin and he was saved.

This is the step you must take if you want to be where Geoffrey is just now. John 1v12 says 'As many as received him to them gave he power to become the sons of God even to them that believe on his name'. It is not what Church you go to, or the good works which you have done, but as a sinner you have got to receive Christ and put your trust, not in the works you do, but in the work done at Calvary which is the answer to your need. Through a coffee-bar in Ballymena, Geoffrey was brought to that place. After he had received Christ he went on to *enjoy Christ*. He found in him what he had been searching for. Christ brought to him real life, as anyone who knew

Geoffrey could see. It's only in Christ that you will find what you are searching for. Man has a spiritual dimension. Man was made for fellowship with God. There is a void in your life which only Christ can fill. Geoffrey also *served Christ*. I don't think you can really appreciate how much we owed to him here in Glenarm. Following the coffee-bar here there were many young people in need of leadership and guidance. This Geoffrey constantly sought to provide. I could never express the gratitude which many of them feel toward him for his counsel and encouragement. So Geoffrey was without Christ, then there was a day when he received Christ, he enjoyed Christ and served Christ and now – glorious fact – he is *with Christ* rejoicing in his presence – and one day those who know his Saviour will be with him too.

Where is Geoffrey Mills? Oh I know he's absent with regard to his family and friends and, yes, he's with Christ with regard to his soul and spirit, but let us also remember that HE IS STILL HERE WITH REGARD TO HIS INFLUENCE. As Geoffrey's employer Mr. Wright has said, 'The most fitting memorial for Geoffrey would be if from this meeting there went out a bunch of young men and women to serve the Lord as Geoffrey served him'. In Ezekiel 22v30 we read, 'And I sought for a man among them, that should make up the hedge, and stand in the gap before me for the land, that I should not destroy it: but I found none'. He needs us to be the influence which Geoffrey was. Will he find none? Geoffrey's experience speaks to you who are not saved too. If it had been you instead of him who set out that night and never came back where would you be? Hell? Are you ready to go? Ready for God's eternity? You can be ready! Let me show you the way. The Bible says first of all that you must **Come to God's appointed place** – Calvary – i.e., you must come to understand the cross and what was accomplished for you there. The Bible makes it clear that 'Without shedding of blood is no remission of sin' (Heb. 9v22). You have sinned for Romans 3v23 states 'All have sinned'. Sin separates from a Holy God and brings you down to hell for Romans 6v23 says 'The wages of sin is death' – the second death too (Revelation 20v4) 'Which is the lake of fire'. Now many people have the mistaken idea that although they have sinned and face judgment, yet somehow by the life they live, the Church they go to, or the works they do they can atone for it and be accepted. This is not so. Remember Hebrews 9 again 'Without shedding of blood, no remission'. You could not atone – it took Christ to atone, and he has, perfectly, at Calvary. You must come to see that the cross is all you need; he has paid and there is nothing left for you to do.

Not only must you come to God's appointed place, Calvary, but you must **Come in God's appointed way** – repentance and faith. You must turn from your sin, for God is holy; you must put your trust for eternity in the work of Christ for you upon the cross; you must receive Christ and let him come into the very centre of your life. That's the way of Salvation, God's way and the only way. You want to be saved? You come in God's appointed way and finally you must **Come in God's appointed time**. In 2 Cor. 6v2 we read 'now is the accepted time, now is the day of salvation'. In Genesis 27v2 Isaac said, 'I know not the day of my death'. Neither do you. That's why now is the time to be saved. In Luke 12 we read of a rich farmer who said, 'I have much goods laid up for many years'. He was counting upon 'many years' but God said unto him, 'Thou fool, this night thy soul shall be required of thee'. How long are you counting upon? You do not know what a day may bring forth and there is no coming back! You are in danger of being lost through a long eternity! Lost in hell! Seek the Saviour now, for now is the only moment you can really be sure of.

We do not know why Geoffrey was taken but we trust God when we do not understand. Yet we know that through his home-call many have been brought to Christ. What about you? My friend before it is too late, before your soul is lost in hell, see that the cross is all you need, turn to Christ in repentance, faith and surrender, receive Him and prove that he can save and save you now.

So we can learn from Jesus' teaching in Luke 12v13-21 about the one who was concerned that his brother should divide the inheritance with him, this parable of the rich fool. Yes, the farmer was astute in certain ways, to some extent a forward planner – pulling down barns to store more and thinking of his later life when he could retire BUT really just a fool. There were three reasons: HE THOUGHT ONLY OF THIS WORLD AND NOT THE WORLD TO COME (just his farm, his food, his earthly future but not his soul or eternity); HE WAS RECKONING UPON MANY YEARS WHEN HE ONLY HAD 'THIS NIGHT, v19-20'. HE HAD MANY RICHES BUT WAS NOT 'RICH TOWARD GOD, v21'. One remembers the need for all of us to be 'rich in faith', James 2v5; we are sinners but can know his pardon by our trust in Christ through whose death God can forgive us, bring us into a relationship with himself and an unfailing inheritance.

Fellowship in the Gospel and Glenarm Church Plant
My '75 diary has a number of references to Glenarm throughout the whole year as I returned again and again to help confirm the young believers in the faith.

The net was cast widely in those days with missions in Portaferry Town Hall, Bloomfield Baptist, Douglas, Isle of Man, Killaughy Mission Hall, Portrush Baptist Church, Carnalbanagh Orange Hall, Rathfriland Tent Mission, Castlereagh Baptist, Glencairn Estate, Knockconney, Poyntzpass Baptist, Cookstown Baptist, Kilrea Tent Mission, Haypark Baptist, Great Victoria Street Baptist (where I received a 'welcome home' from Pastor Hugh Orr one Sunday evening) and Upperlands.

Glenarm stands out in my memory at that time – especially the formation of the church. I had travelled the road to Glenarm often, as noted, from Magherafelt in my years of ministry there; then we came by a different way later from Newtownards. It was during the latter time that the church was formed. The following is the short summary of the beginnings entered in the front of the minute book of the Church (included by kind permission).

FORMATION OF GLENARM BAPTIST CHURCH:
For nine years, services were held from time to time by Mr. Morrow and friends in his café in Altmore Street. A regular Gospel Meeting was commenced and the Youth Work which was begun grew until large numbers were attending. Many professed conversion and concern was felt that something more permanent should be established for them where they could be instructed and cared for.

Following a three week mission, conducted by Pastor Hamilton Moore in the newly renovated hall at Mr. Morrow's, a meeting of all interested people was held in May 1976 to discuss the formation of a New Testament Church in Glenarm. Sixteen people attended the meeting and fourteen expressed their willingness to join such a church if it was constituted. Mr. Moore promised to do all he could to assist the fellowship over the first number of months.

On the following Sunday morning the church was formed. At the commencement of the meeting Pastor Moore extended the right hand of fellowship to the fourteen who were willing to join and commended them to the Lord in Prayer.

A witness for the Gospel had been established on the east coast of Antrim. It was to continue to grow in the following years. And during 1976, the Lord did a wonderful thing for us as a family. On 10th November Eileen gave birth to my son, David Hamilton.

During those years of evangelism, I continued to work for my GCSEs and 'A' Levels. I also approached Dr Oakley who was Principal of the Baptist College and he encouraged me to enrol in his Elementary Greek Class which met five mornings a week. He explained that the secret of learning Greek was 'little and often' and if I could get to some of the classes weekly I would soon pick up the language. Could I come back home week by week the night before to attend? My attitude to College study was beginning to change.

What can I say about these opportunities in mission in many different churches and the blessing God poured out from place to place? God graciously worked in hearts by his Spirit. I have learned and am still learning to let God lead. In John 5, Jesus has given us an example. In v19 Jesus can state, 'The Son can do nothing of himself, but what he seeth the Father do: for what things soever he doeth, these also doeth the Son likewise'. Jesus did not initiate his ministry. He sought to do whatever God was doing, how God was working and let the Father work through him. We must learn to do the same. In going out to serve God we must not simply seek to work for God but seek to put ourselves in his hands and let him work through us. Let God set the agenda; find out what God is doing and submit to him so that he might do it through you.

As a family we resided in West Winds Estate for over three years, with my travels taking me to Belgium, France, England, Scotland and also the more familiar route, back to Glenarm. I maintained my studies by correspondence and, as encouraged by Dr. Oakley, often dropped into the College on Sandown Road for Greek on Monday mornings on my way to some mission in the evening; also I would return home Tuesday night for Wednesday morning and Thursday night for Friday morning in College – the language was kept up by this means. I must confess that driving along the road I had got to know a substantial part of the book (J. W. Wenham[21]) so well that I could recite the declensions, the conjugations and a lot of the vocabulary from memory.

The people in the cul-de-sac were friendly and we had formed a good relationship. I believe that our lives and the witness we bore will have told for eternity. It was a dangerous place with unpleasant incidents; our next door neighbour was beaten up for very little reason. I often was leaving to stay in different places sometimes only getting home a number of nights in any particular month. I recall my concern for my family – what would happen while I was away? Yet God spoke to me on one occasion enabling me to trust him. It was during a short holiday in Portrush in July when the CWU Convention was taking place. The arrangement for this particular day was that I would attend the morning Bible Study while Wendy and David were taken to the beach by their Mum. I remember hearing Willie Mullan preach on Isa. 49v15-16. I have often preached on the chapter since. There is SOMETHING HISTORICAL here. The initial context will be the exiles in Babylon and Isaiah speaking prophetically to them in their trouble and great distress. There is also SOMETHING CHRISTOLOGICAL here, for the Servant of the Lord is here – not just Israel for in v6 the Servant has a ministry to Israel and a great future for his people. BUT there is also SOMETHING PRACTICAL HERE, God's care of his people and his reassurances to them. In v13-14 God comforts his people who lament in their situation, 'The Lord hath forsaken me, and my Lord hath forgotten me'. From then until now the people of God have often felt this. But it is not true. So here God reassures his people that they are (1) IN HIS MIND. 'Can a woman forget her sucking child, that she should not have compassion on the son of her womb? Yea, they may forget, yet will I not forget thee'. They are also (2) graven ON HIS HANDS. 'Behold, I have graven thee upon the palms of my hands'. Not just written on his hands, like a reminder or stamped but graven.

There is permanency here. We are always remembered. Finally, and this is the statement which meant so much to me at that time. We are (3) BEFORE HIS EYES. 'Thy walls are continually before me'. This was the preacher's emphasis that morning. I could go away without fear for the Lord was watching over my wife and little family. Another verse was also precious and reassuring to me – Exodus 34v24, 'For I will cast out the nations before thee, and enlarge thy borders: neither shall any man desire thy land when thou shalt go up to appear before the Lord thy God thrice in the year'. No greater protection could we have.

During our time in Newtownards as noted earlier, my precious mother went home to be with the Lord. A secondary tumour from terminal cancer had occurred, this time inoperable. I was speaking at a Children's Camp in Bangor (children from Ballee Baptist Church, Ballymena) in the mornings, but was able to spend time with her in the hospital in Newtownards in the afternoons and evenings. In John 14v1 Jesus assures his disciples, 'Let not your heart be troubled: you believe in God, believe also in me'. But what is the Secret of the Untroubled Heart? First FAITH IN HEAVEN. It is an actual place – 'My Father's house', with 'many abodes'. There is a real heaven and an actual hell. There is a place prepared for a prepared people. Then there is FAITH IN CHRIST'S COMING. 'If I go ... I will come again, and receive you unto myself'. Nothing is more sure than this. He will return actually, bodily and physically – as it is affirmed in Acts 1v11 and 1 Thess. 4v16-18. Here is a promise which can dry our tears. But finally to be untroubled about the future we need to be sure that we have our FAITH IN CHRIST – Christ as the way. 'Thomas saith unto him...how can we know the way? Jesus saith unto him, I am the way, the truth and the life: no man cometh unto the Father but by me'. He was going to leave his disciples but he would go home by the way of the cross – to be the substitute for sinners, to do all that needed to be done for them to be no longer rejected but accepted by God (on the cross he cried 'It is Finished!' John 19v30). They were at a DISTANCE from God, separated, alienated from God in their rebellion and disobedience – but he was the way; they were in DARKNESS about God and the truth – but he was the truth, the living embodiment of God and he was the one who could enlighten them about the way of salvation; they were DEAD spiritually to

God – but he was the one who could regenerate them, they can be born again and have eternal life. So through the cross he opened up the way for all who will trust in him rather than in themselves. This my mother had done many years earlier. She had a peace and serenity at the last born out of a close relationship with God. When the ambulance men came to take her from Ballyhalbert to the Hospital – that last journey – she witnessed all the way to them! Jesus had said 'that where I am, there you may be also'. And so it was.

Monkstown Baptist Church

The time came when we responded to a call from Monsktown Baptist Church to become pastor there. The induction service was held in September 1977. The church had acquired a house in Ballyduff Road, Carnmoney, (formally Campbell's farm). The Kernoghan Brothers, Alan, Tommy and Richard with their father Billy had undertaken to complete all the work that was necessary to make it a comfortable home and were still finishing it off. So Mrs Bingham, 'Bingie' as she was affectionately called, who lived in King's Drive off the Doagh Road kindly vacated her home for us until we could move up to Ballyduff.

Those years in Monkstown were blessed years. God was moving in a special way. The church had come through periods of difficulty but now a new chapter was beginning. A Converts' Class was started for those who came to faith. Brother Billy Kernoghan the church secretary and I took the lead in it. Some of those who attended even learned to read while they were attending. Billy had a great heart for God's people and especially for those who were new to the faith. How he brought so much encouragement to them! At the Induction Service my father had said to him (unknown to me), 'Look after young Timothy'. He always remembered that appeal and on many occasions brought wise counsel and genuine support.

Traditional missions were held in Monkstown in those years, also coffee bars, cottage meetings, and meetings like the Morning Break which still continues. We were blessed with help from the visits of preachers such as the former Pastor, Val English or Pastor Tom McNabb and others. I often gave one day a week to visit around the doors in the Monkstown estate. The Holy

Spirit was at work. I recall that even one Sunday morning a young lady who lived in the estate a stone's throw from the church was compelled of the Spirit to leave her seat and walk up to the front to seek the Lord. (I saw her recently at a funeral in the church, still going on with God). There were other notable conversions – a former UVF leader who got on fire for the Lord. He would bring his work mates to 100 Ballyduff Road where they could have lunch. But the strategy was that he and I would talk. He would ask questions about the Bible; I would answer – but of course there was a 'captive' listening audience!! His conversion not only made an impact on his work mates but his whole family, as Christ was now head of the home. While living at Ballyduff, Wendy and David welcomed a new little sister into our home, Pamela Joy; my youngest daughter was born on 11 February, 1978 – this was to be our family.

Student Days and Glenarm
The motivation to complete a Degree in Theology really began back in 1974 before moving out from Magherafelt again into evangelism. As explained, I had enrolled in Correspondence Courses with the London Bible College and Wolsey Hall to take GCSEs and 'A' levels, plus attending the Irish Baptist College for my Elementary Greek. Over the next few years these exams were sat in different places, in the Technical Colleges in Newtownards, Newcastle and Belfast. The more I considered the situation I realised that to complete the BD by Correspondence was going to take a serious amount of time. I came to the conviction that I would have to go to the College full-time rather than continue for many years by correspondence. The situation had to be shared with the office bearers in Monkstown. One of them in particular encouraged me to proceed if I felt it was God's way forward for me. So I resigned from the church in 1980 and at the beginning of the summer, as soon as I could, I moved out of 100 Ballyduff Road. In the providence of God, Glenarm Baptist, were very open for me to come to live in the village and assist them. While they could not take on a Pastor full-time, we lived on my grant for study and they supported me during the summer. So we came to the church I had helped to plant. We were to move into the house in Glenarm which the church had been renovating and during this time

stayed in Aughagash. Sister Agnes McCalmont lovingly loaned her home to us for as long as needed until we could finish our place of residence in Glenarm.

Things had progressed quickly concerning my leading to study in the College. My application was positive because of the 'A' levels I had successfully taken. The Letter of acceptance from the Admissions Officer, Mr. S.M. Wisener had a sentence stating that the offer had become 'unconditional' and that 'it will be up to the faculty to decide whether or not you should be admitted to first BD or second BD'. Actually, I was able to skip the first year, the Arts year, going into year two because I also was allowed to take Queen's Examinations in Philosophy (Scholastic Philosophy and the Philosophy of Religion), plus Elementary NT Greek. These opened the door fully to me into the second year and to begin serious study. So the young man of twenty two who was uneasy with the encouragement in the Letter of invitation to the pastorate in Magherafelt to seek help from the College (as per the advice of Pastor Boggs) ended up as a full-time student of IBC after fourteen years in the ministry. It was September 1980.

Glenarm was a special place for our children to live. Glenarm Forest, the river with the salmon returning to spawn, the Castle, the beach and finally, the two-teacher Primary School. Our children loved it. I worked hard to get the house completed. Finally, it was finished – a new kitchen, three bedrooms, a large lounge which could double up as a church crèche on Sundays for the many children who attended, just across from Mr Morrow's where the church met.

I travelled daily from Glenarm to the College in Sandown Road. There was some pressure in travelling – especially since during September I also conducted an Evangelistic Mission in Lisburn Baptist Church. But from time to time brother Eddie Rea (later to be a well-known pastor) who also was enrolled came all the way from Ballyclare (a huge detour) to drive me to Sandown Road.

When I began to study in IBC, one or two of the students asked me why having 'arrived' and been a pastor for twelve years I came to study in the College. My response was that I needed to deepen my knowledge of the Bible, to learn the original languages, and to gain in my understanding as to how to handle many of the pastoral problems which were now more open that formerly. Also there are many challenges we face today from modern scholarship seeking to undermine the faith of some – especially our high view of Scripture; areas in Christology etc. I wished to be more competent for the Lord in every way. So my journey in theology had begun. To sum up my College years, I got to know God at a deeper level.

The years in Glenarm were special years teaching in a young church plant, laying foundations for the believers. Just recently, at a reunion meeting to thank God for the Coffee Bar held in the café forty years earlier I was moved when someone produced a little guide I had taught them as young people about how to witness and especially the steps in pointing someone to Christ. They had never forgotten. In those days the church grew in numbers and its witness to the truth of the gospel became more influential. It also took the decision to become part of the Association of Baptist Churches in Ireland. Its witness was crucial in that part of north east Antrim. I remember sitting in the kitchen of Margaret's Café telling a young lady, perturbed or likely convicted about what she had been hearing from me in preaching (John 3v1-7, the story of Nicodemus 'ye must be born again!'). I insisted that I would take her to meet other ministers of her own denomination who would affirm the absolute necessity of this experience – although for many years no such message had been preached with the same clarity locally. Thankfully in grace God opened her eyes along with many others.

In Northern Ireland there are quite a number of different approaches to worship among Baptist Churches. Some have given great prominence to the Lord's Supper in their morning services by making it more central; others less, even not celebrating it every Sunday. In Glenarm the decision was taken to celebrate it (weekly of course) first in open worship followed by the preached word. Similarly baptismal services were held from time to time, demonstrating the truth of believers' baptism by immersion. These were meant to 'model' the simplicity of the early church recounted by Luke in the Acts of the Apostles. My years in Glenarm, living among the people were years of important influence. It gave out the message that the church was there to stay and that it would continue to be an influence for good among the people and for God and his glory.

Is that the Phone?

The years of intensive study did not end with graduation from the College in July 1983. I continued my ministry in Glenarm but also felt constrained to begin Postgraduate Study – study of course which did not require travelling so frequently to Belfast. At this point I had no idea of the significance of my commitment to study for the future. All I knew was the compulsion from God to continue. The work in Glenarm was progressing and the opportunity came for moving things forward from its base in Mr Morrow's. There were two amazingly significant developments within just a couple of years. A substantial building in Glenarm which dated back to the eighteenth century sat on the corner of Toberwine Street and Castle Street. It had recently served as the Courthouse but became available for purchase. One evening, it was quite late, when the children were already in bed, there was a surprise telephone call from Mr. David Hamill, Secretary of Magherafelt at the time. A meeting of the church had been called to appoint elders, but apparently a letter had been sent, to which members could reply. They had been asked to also express their thoughts concerning the need of a pastor for the church. Quite a few mentioned my name. Something which is usually unprecedented took place. A short time earlier a brother, a deacon from Magherafelt, had met me on the street in Glenarm. He had asked me about returning to South Derry – I do not remember my reply. That night the same brother pressed the church to issue a call. Remarkably, the vote was substantial and hence the telephone call from David. Out of the blue, with no previous consultation, or discussion I was faced with the challenge of returning to minister in Magherafelt.

I took some time to prayerfully reflect on the situation. Eventually I reached my decision to respond positively to the call. From every point of view it seemed to be the way forward. This freed the Glenarm church from any financial burden of pastoral support at that time, making it easier to secure and prepare the Courthouse building for the church. The following year in Glenarm on 27th July 1985 a gathering of approximately two hundred people came to the official opening. Included are a few lines from the Irish Baptist Magazine which reported the event:

> The opening ceremony was conducted by Pastor H. Moore (Magherafelt) and the building was declared open by one of the senior members of the

church, Mr. Norman Huston. Pastor J.R. Grant (B.U.O.I. Secretary) was the chairman for the opening service and the Union President, Mr S. N. Hamilton, read the scriptures and prayed. A brief history of the building, which dated back to the eighteenth century...and a history of the Baptist witness in Glenarm were brought by Leslie Morrow (church secretary). Pastor S. Carson was the speaker...and commenced a two week mission on Monday 29th July.

The work in Glenarm had moved on to a building in which much could be attempted for the witness of the Gospel for the years to come.

How you have Grown!
As a family we received a warm welcome back to Magherafelt; back to the same church building on the Ballyronan Road; back to the same house at Moneymore Road (altered in some ways during our absence); back to the same loving members but after ten years of absence, children now grown up, young people matured.

I remember the first sermon I preached on my return to Magherafelt. John 1v29-51 – the theme was on Discipleship in John. I referred to the nature of John's Gospel and quoted from Clement of Alexandria (c 155-215)[22], 'Last of all, John, perceiving that the external facts had been made plain ... being urged by his friends, and inspired by the Holy Spirit, composed a spiritual Gospel'. I proceeded to show that John has at the beginning of his Gospel outlined what discipleship really involves. First, John reminds us that discipleship begins by BEHOLDING JESUS AS THE LAMB OF GOD, v29-37. We have not started for heaven or as disciples until we grasp that we needed a lamb; we are sinners without hope apart from what Christ has done at Calvary. Our sin has closed heaven's door to us. Jesus insists in John 8v21, 'ye ... shall die in your sins: whither I go, ye cannot come'. But Jesus was the LAMB FROM GOD and FOR GOD. In other words, when we could do absolutely nothing to get right with God, he himself in love took the initiative to remove his own wrath by sending his son. We need to believe the good news, turn from our rebellion/independence from God, trust in Christ alone for our salvation. Only then do we begin our path as disciples. Secondly, discipleship involves FOLLOWING JESUS, v37 'They followed Jesus'; v43 'Jesus ... findeth Philip, and saith to him "follow me"'. Following Jesus means allegiance to his person and submission to his teaching. Are we faithful to him, confessing him and submitting to his teaching in the word of God? Again discipleship involves ABIDING IN JESUS, v39 'They came and saw where he dwelt, and abode (the word is *menō* used again in John 15v4 'Abide in me, and I in you') with him that day'. We need power to follow as a disciple; that power or enabling comes from maintaining a vital living relationship with Christ. But there is more to discipleship. It also means that we will seek to FIND OTHERS AND BRING THEM TO JESUS, v40-42. John highlights the ministry of Andrew, Simon Peter's brother. In John he is always finding others and bringing them to Jesus, 1v42, his brother; 6v8-9, the lad with five loaves and two fish; 12v20-23, the inquiring Greeks. Do we find others and bring them to Jesus? Andrew was always in the background – Peter was the one who took the lead and so preached on Pentecost and at the Beautiful Gate, that first, three thousand and then five thousand turned to the Lord (Acts 2v41; 4v4). But Andrew had first brought him to Christ! Disciples are soul winners. Lastly, they are those who DO WHATEVER HE SAYS, 2v5, 'Whatever he saith unto you, do it'. The 'week' of discipleship which began in John 1v29 carries through into chapter two here. To be true disciples we must be prepared to go wherever he sends and do whatever he commands. This was basically my first sermon on that particular Sunday.

One man in the congregation that morning was Pastor Boggs. He was now retired from ministry in Tobermore and Carndaisy but often came to Magherafelt in the morning. He commented as he left that from the quotations of the Early Fathers, the insights, and just generally how I preached, that there had been evident improvement from the man who moved away in 1974. I always valued the opinions of the man who chaired the first church meeting when I was first called to the church in 1968; the man who encouraged the church to include the reference to 'seeking the help of the College' sixteen years earlier.

Ministry in Magherafelt 1984 – 1990

The next six years were special years of ministry. There had been periods of turbulence in recent years and the number of office bearers was small. They were happy for me to take the initiative and give a positive lead. Everyone welcomed the opening of a new chapter.

The opportunities were many in sharing the gospel, as I was still involved in mission outreach in the whole district and beyond. In addition, a meeting held for children in the local Primary School exceeded all expectations with up to 100 children permitted to attend weekly. Brother Tommy Loughrey, Pastor Boggs, brother Des Buchanan of Child Evangelism Fellowship and Denver Michaels, now Pastor of Cullybackey Elim Church, helped me grasp the opportunity. Children involved in GCSE RE in St. Pius Secondary School and in the Convent School for Girls were able to learn what Baptists believe about baptism and the celebration of the Lord's Supper. But second time around I would suggest that my ministry had a different emphasis; preaching was centred around consolidation and encouragement rather than exhortation and rebuke. I am reminded that in the prophecy of Isaiah the prophet himself received two basic commissions. In Isaiah 6 he hears the voice of the Lord speaking 'Whom shall I send and who will go for us?' Isaiah responds 'Here am I, send me', (Isaiah 6v8-9). He was sent to preach a message of repentance and of course as we know the people hardened their hearts – hence the future exile to Babylon. In chapter(s) 39-40 the book moves forward prophetically to the time of the exile – see Isaiah 39 v6-8. Isaiah now receives a new commission; Isaiah 40v1 brings to us God's call to Isaiah 'Comfort ye, comfort ye my people, saith your God'. Isaiah was called to a ministry of comfort because of the distress and despair the people in exile would experience. He was to emphasise to them over and over again in the chapters that followed that their God saw them where they were and knew their situation and had not forgotten them. For example, Isaiah 40v27-28 states, 'Why sayest thou, O Jacob, and speakest O Israel, My way is hid from the Lord, and my judgment is passed over from my God? Hast thou not known? Hast thou not heard, that the everlasting God, the Lord, the Creator of the ends of the earth, fainteth not, neither is weary? There is no searching of his understanding'. The message was that God was not limited by TIME, he was the everlasting God; not limited by SPACE, he was the creator of the ends of the earth; not limited by EFFORT, he did not faint and he was not limited in his KNOWLEDGE of all that is. Looking to such a God would strengthen them in their difficult circumstances for he was a God who gives power to the faint.

Often young Pastors in their zeal for the glory of God and desire to see their church grow can end up engaging in a ministry of correction and rebuke. If this is the tone Sunday after Sunday as they wield the rod or the whip those who are weak or struggling with certain problems can become discouraged, even depressed. You will notice that they are missing, why? They cannot bear such a constant emphasis. Experience taught me this. The Lord's people need encouragement. The care of God our shepherd is emphasised in Isaiah 40v11, 'He shall feed his flock like a shepherd: he shall gather the lambs with his arm, and carry them in his bosom, and shall gently lead those that are with young'. This pastoral care needs to be evident in the pulpit as well. Again, in visitation the same pastoral counselling is vital. Satan has no mercy and when sickness comes or terminal illness the saints of God need reassurance from God's word. I remember the elder I met in 1967 at Easter in the Believers' Meetings in the Grosvenor Hall when I was coming to South Derry for the first time. He was a man who often had preached standing at the Diamond in Magherafelt. But when he became seriously ill at the last, he was troubled with fears and doubt. I came to realise that in ministering to him and others like him that it is the plain texts about the cross, the work of Christ and the assurances of Scripture that need to be read.

Looking back on the first series I preached in Magherafelt on I John, it was providentially the ministry needed for that time. John's first epistle is about the tests of life. Some had left the church, influenced by what they thought was new knowledge, now referred to as 'gnostic insights' (I John 2v19). The idea was that 'the flesh' was inherently evil and that within man there was a divine spark that needed again to become aware of its true home. Some claimed that they had been granted special insight or knowledge of this and therefore despised others as second class Christians, particularly the people left behind in the church. The challenge of I John was 'do we really know God?' or 'are we truly born again, truly children of God?' Basically the book is about RIGHT BELIEF or do we believe that Jesus Christ really came in the flesh, became incarnate? 1 John 4v3 affirms that 'Every spirit that confesseth not that Jesus Christ is come in the flesh, is not of God'. Christ's mediatorship for us requires that he is truly man to take our place. Again RIGHT BEHAVIOUR. God is light, perfectly holy and so we do not really know him if we are daily yielding ourselves to sin and indulging the flesh. Finally, RIGHT RELATIONSHIP WITH ONE ANOTHER; the challenge is that since 'God is love' (1 John 4v8) we ought to love one another and accept one another. This also is a sign of new birth.

One passage which sums up the latter is I John 4v7-19. This was an emphasis made back in 1984. In verse 8 we have THE AFFIRMATION OF GOD'S LOVE. 'He that loveth not knoweth not God; for God is love'. God is love in his nature or his innermost being. Love is inherent within God. V9-11 show us THE MANIFESTATION OF GOD'S LOVE. He sent his Son. His love was active, seen in concerned actions, sacrificial and uncaused by anything in others. 'Herein is love, not that we loved God but that he loved us…' Since God manifested such love – uncaused by anything in us, in fact in spite of animosity or hostility so we should also manifest such love to others. In v12 we read of THE PERFECTION OF GOD'S LOVE. 'His love is perfected in us'. This is the sensational message here. IN THE PAST God's love was manifested in sending his Son. But what about today? IN THE PRESENT God's love is manifested through our love. God's Love is PERFECTED ONLY when it is reproduced in us! Our life of love manifesting at times the same love, uncaused by anything in the other person, is a constant sermon on the love of God. Again, v17 emphasises that while Jesus is no longer in the world, we, God's children, are. God's love ought to be seen through us as it was in the past demonstrated through Christ. This is a serious challenge. Are we manifesting God's love in and through us?

During these years my Postgraduate work continued. I completed my Master of Theology degree, four three-hour examinations and a 20,000 word thesis. The thesis was entitled 'The Influence of Jewish Concepts in New Testament Apocalyptic' – not as complicated as it sounds – and was typed on a small typewriter by Eileen. But I was not finished. I still felt compelled to continue my studies. At first it appeared that there were no local supervisors available. Did this mean that I must enrol in the London Bible College, where I had started my work by correspondence all those years ago? At last Professor Ted Russell (Principal of Union Theological College, Belfast) was willing to take me on. So once again, I was working first in pastoral care of the church plus using every other moment available to engage in my research.

The Pieces of the Jigsaw fit!
It is demanding to be involved in PhD studies and yet keep caring for the people of God in a church context. My strategy was to use mainly the 'free' weeks i.e., when someone else was coming to preach on a Sunday or a midweek, I could ease up on preparing new messages and focus on my thesis again. Of course such intense study, reading yourself back into where you were working, was difficult. Sometimes I would stop and say to myself. 'Why are you doing all this? What is the point? These church members were happy with you when you were here the first time. Why put yourself through all this stress?' But I felt compelled to keep going. Then things started to develop in unexpected ways.

I was involved in some teaching for the College, before I moved from Glenarm, a course on 'Evangelistic Preaching'. On one occasion Dr. Oakley arranged for a student from Ballymena who was accepted for College study to come down to meet with me in Glenarm over the summer to get him started on his Hellenistic Greek. That student was Dr David Luke, now Postgraduate Director and Historical Theology Tutor. Time was moving on and I had been in Magherafelt for a number of years. But the situation was about to change in IBC.

The time came when it was clear that Dr. Oakley who served the College from 1974-1988 would move with his wife Esme to Scotland to become Principal of the Scottish College. In conversation with him, he expressed the hope that I would consider following him in IBC as New Testament teacher. I believe he also expressed this in the 'official circles'. But of course he was informed that it was not possible for him to appoint his successor! My mind began to think of the needs of the College. Then things moved forward in ways which I could not have foreseen. An announcement appeared in the Irish Baptist Magazine for a new Principal! I would be willing to consider helping in New Testament but NOT to become Principal!

I recall one occasion as I was considering all this, Pastor Boggs called at the Manse. I expressed to him the fact I was aware of the need in the College for a New Testament lecturer and of course he encouraged me to go forward. We were sitting close to the old church building on the Moneymore Road where as I have mentioned already, many years earlier he had encouraged the church not just to issue a call to me but to include a statement about seeking any help from the College I could receive! The last week for applications arrived and just before the deadline closed I put my name on the table.

I remember the night of the interview. It was held in the Moyola Lodge, Castledawson. Eileen and I shared a meal with the board and then I met them on my own. I recall it was a particularly intense interview – I was exhausted by the time it was over and I drove home. Within a few days a call came from Pastor Grant, Union Secretary. The decision was that the Interviewing Committee was offering me the post of New Testament lecturer in IBC, and would offer the post of Principal to another applicant. A response was needed later that day! My wife Eileen initially felt I should decline the offer. But when we discussed it further I explained to her that I had not really sought the Principalship. My burden was to help the College in whatever way I could. The decision was made. Later that day I replied positively to the offer. They were delighted. Everything was working out as the Committee had planned. BUT ... I did not forsee that when the post of Principal was offered to the other candidate he actually declined it! I recall a couple of weeks later, as I came from Magherafelt to deliver a lecture in IBC, the Chairman of the Committee, James Greenwood, who was also Principal of Stranmillis, asked me to call. He wanted to discuss the way the Committee perceived we should go forward. The proposal was that the College Secretary N.A. Shields would become Principal for one year and I would be Principal Designate. The year would give me time to work with Norman and get acquainted with the demands and challenges of the Principalship. In this way my reservations about taking on this responsibility were assuaged.

I could now see the reason for all the commitment to study from those early years in Magherafelt in 1974. My course through GCSEs and 'A' level study, to degree and MTh study, and finally to the PhD had been a long road. But the pieces of the jigsaw were beginning to fit together. I never would have had the opportunity to serve in IBC or later to have a role in Emanuel University, Romania without this pilgrimage. 'My father planned it all'.

(C) Hamilton Moore – Principal of IBC

Principal with New Team Members

I was appointed Principal of the Irish Baptist College on 21st September 1990 at the Commencement Service. Pastor John Birnie was also appointed as full-time Secretary and Pastor Billy Colville, at that time in Dundonald Baptist Church, took on part-time the role of Tutor with responsibility for OT studies. Other members of College staff, as Dr. Maurice Dowling, Dr. Philip Johnston, Mr Paddy Roche, Mrs Kathleen Johnston, gave us a warm welcome. I had served one year from 1989 as NT lecturer alongside N.A. Shields from whom I had learned so much down the years. I continued to live in Magherafelt during that first year, travelling every day, leaving at 7.15 am, returning most evenings around 6.30 pm, preaching in the Church and carrying on pastoral ministry. Things were quite demanding, especially as so many lectures needed to be prepared; but God helped me.

We were obliged as a family to move from Magherafelt to the Principal's House on Sandown Road, adjacent to the College. During the summer of 1990 we had to say farewell to our friends in the church where I had opportunity to serve for twelve years in total. We moved in July to give us time to settle into our new home, organise schooling etc. The few months also gave me time to finish my PhD on 'The Book of the Revelation and Contemporary Apocalypses' in order to present it by September 15th, just ahead of the recognition of my role as Principal.

'Daddy's Boys'

What is the significance of this sub heading? It came about through a brief encounter one afternoon as a student from the College came over to see me in my home on some matter. I was overheard by my children, Wendy, David and Pamela addressing him 'Come in, son'. They joked with me about the greeting and from that moment the students were described as 'Daddy's Boys!' But of course the point really was that they had detected my deep interest and support for all the students and my commitment to their success, a goal which of course was shared by the other faculty members. I recall on one occasion a few years later when the College had moved to Moira, the Hellenistic Greek classes had been running for a few months. Some of the students were beginning to struggle with the language. I commented, 'I will get you through this course or die trying!' They knew that they had my total support and the determination to see them succeed. Personally I felt a great sense of fulfilment in the work of the College and this was to continue for twenty years.

Castlereagh Baptist
Castlereagh invited me to preach a few Sundays in the summer of 1990. My relationship with them went back over many years and especially to the mission I had with them in 1975. Having moved to East Belfast with my family it was important to find a spiritual home. Two of my children were now teenagers – the third one soon to be – and there were young people in Castlereagh of similar age. So Castlereagh became our home church and I continued to preach for them on various Sundays and Thursdays at their Prayer Meeting. They were happy to have regular ministry, with the understanding that if the Lord directed them to seek a full-time pastor I would be willing and happy to allow the church to move forward into a situation where they would receive better pastoral care. One attempt at finding a full time pastor was not successful and so I continued until 1992. It was at this point that the Elders approached me again with the proposal that they wished to formalise the arrangement with me and to confirm that I would continue 'officially' as part time pastor for the foreseeable future. The arrangement was to last for fourteen happy years. I believe that the regular ministry kept the church together. As far as I was concerned it was good to be as it were 'at the coal face', relating directly with people who needed teaching, encouragement and comfort. There was pressure at times, especially in preparing for the Thursday Prayer Meeting and the Sundays; also with coming home on Sunday evening not to relax but to face preparing for five lectures the next day. But God sustained me. It was during this period that my father, who had been living with us for some months, peacefully went home to be with the Lord in his sleep on 12th October 1991. In the latter years of his life, his thoughtful ministry and insightful wisdom were much appreciated by the assembly in Ballyhalbert. A quiet, unassuming gentleman who left a legacy of service behind. Throughout my ministry his constant words of encouragement were a real source of blessing to me.

A Workman seeking not to be Ashamed

My preaching had changed somewhat over the years. It was more allegorical in the early days. I had gradually learned – with of course also benefiting from the guidance of Dr. Oakley in his class on Homiletics – how to more 'rightly divide the word of God'. Walter Kaisar, lecturing on hermeneutics, the interpretation of the Scriptures, warned of the dangers of not being diligent in the exposition of many texts in preaching. He quoted the words, 'Wonderful things in the bible I see; some of them put there by you and by me!' It is vital to faithfully bring out the sense of what God is saying in a text or passage, not simply force our own interpretation upon it – making it say what we ourselves want to affirm. Handling God's revelation in this manner is to distort it, perhaps even to deny it.

In my book on *1 & 2 Timothy and Titus* one recalls how Paul exhorted his younger colleague Timothy in 2 Tim. 2v14-16 about the appropriate handling of the word of God[23]. Timothy is to do his utmost to engage in a ministry approved by God. He is to be an example of how to have the right approach in handling the Scriptures. His teaching must be profitable and edifying, in contrast to the negative and harmful effects of the useless controversies of the false teachers. Timothy is a 'workman' and as such is to handle the Scriptures with care. 'Rightly dividing' is expressed by a verb which has been used in a number of senses e.g., to cut a straight road, plough a straight furrow, sew a straight seam, to be direct in one's speech. It has the idea here of one who does not deviate from expounding the truth, not just his own ideas. The shame that any workman feels when the incompetence of his work is detected is applied here to the Christian ministry. The Christian teacher should be able to continually submit his work to God for his approval. Here are some basic principles I have tried to apply in endeavouring to rightly divide the word of God.

Excursus: Basic Principles of Interpretation

1. The Biblical scholar insists that the Biblical text first of all means what it originally meant. God's Word to us today is first of all precisely what it was to them.
2. The task is two-fold: find out what the text originally meant and then seek to hear that same meaning in a variety of new and different contexts in our own day.

3. So the aim of good interpretation is to get to the 'plain meaning of the text'. The most important approach in this task is enlightened common sense. See what makes good sense of the text. True hermeneutics brings relief to the mind as well as a challenge to the heart.
4. So the interpreter seeks to understand what was said to them THEN and THERE and hear that same word in the HERE and NOW.

    To do exegesis requires knowledge of many things. This is the reason why being involved in the work of the kingdom demands good preparation of ourselves. I had appreciated the opportunity in the past to be in the Irish Baptist College to acquire 'the tools'. First the biblical language, then word studies, the use of a lexicon where one can select the important words and trace their use either in the OT or NT. Now of course, Bible Works is available. This original languages Bible software program is really useful for Biblical exegesis and research.

    It was helpful to me to gain some competence in textual criticism – checking for variant readings, with one or two translations, or the use of an Interlinear Bible. Then the dictionaries, which help with the background, the occasion of the book, summary of purpose. Finally the commentaries – to grasp the meaning of the verses in their context. A good commentary will list and briefly discuss the various proposed interpretations with reasons for and against.
5. We cannot make the Bible mean anything that we want. The text cannot be interpreted to say something that it never meant to say. The true meaning of the text for us is what God originally intended it to mean when it was first spoken.
6. When we share comparable life situations with the 1st century setting, or an OT setting, God's word to us is the same as his word to them. The moral teaching abides in every culture and every age.

The kind of disputing concerning the truth that Paul goes on to refer to in 2 Tim. 2v16-18 will not build up the believers but in effect can undermine their faith and turn them away from God. This is what is meant by 'increase unto more ungodliness'. Heretical arguments are profane and futile. The dire effect of the spread of false teaching is compared to gangrene, a known medical term from at least the fourth century BC for the decay of flesh in a part of the body which is steadily advancing. The present tense of the imperative 'avoid' means that this is something which Timothy must constantly seek to do. False teaching is both godless and gangrenous. But the true interpretation of a text or passage will build up. This is what I endeavoured to do for the fourteen years of my ministry in Castlereagh.

Romania Comes to Belfast and Vice Versa

During the nineteen-nineties there were a number of Romanians who came to study at the Irish Baptist College. When Nicolae Ceausescu and his wife Elena were assassinated on Christmas day 1989, freedom came to the country of Romania. People could now travel to the west. Before that time only four men were permitted to enter into theological training at the Seminary in Bucharest. But now some came to the Irish Baptist College to study and better prepare themselves to serve their own people. There were young men like Marian Diceanu, Catalin Croitor, Marian Moscivic and Cristi Galatanu, who came to take College Ministry Development Courses and Queen's BD studies; other key people in Romania were enrolled in Postgraduate Courses. George Verzea (the Vice-President of Evangelism Explosion for Europe), Vasile Lucac, (Principal of the Christian High School, Cluj), Pastor Gigi Dobrin (Medias Baptist Church and teacher in Emanuel Baptist University, Oradea), Pastor Marius Sabou (Bethel Baptist Church, Cluj) and Pastor Beni Faragau (Iris Baptist Church, Cluj). These were the first key contacts we made in Romania. Brother Beni actually stayed in Belfast for the most of two semesters – fulfilling the requirements of the University. He was given hospitality by Dr. David Gooding, who in the past had visited Romania and Cluj. There were many opportunities to discuss theology during Beni's stay. But they were both busy men with different responsibilities, Dr. Gooding was involved with his writing of various commentaries and Beni his research for his postgraduate studies. So they devised a means of communication – a blackboard on which could be written various comments and suggestions without having long periods of discussion. Other students came later, as Pastor Ovidiu Hanc (who completed both his MTh and later his PhD and now teaches in Emanuel). I travelled out sometimes to supervise various students in their studies and also was able to enrol others in the Masters with Lampeter University, Wales, enabling them to study in their own country and see them through to a local graduation.

My first trip to the country was by invitation from Slavic Gospel Association, UK[24] in January 2001. On the way out I met a SGA teacher at Heathrow and we travelled together to the home of Charles Ficsor (Good News Foundation) in Orgovany, Hungary. Unexpectedly he became ill and, exercising care for him pastorally, SGA arranged for him to return to the airport and fly home. I was expected to return with him, but requested to continue on alone. So on my first trip I travelled to Oradea and to Medias and taught the courses myself over the next two weeks. This was the first of many opportunities I was privileged to be given by SGA. I recall one occasion standing outside the Emanuel Baptist Church in Oradea and being asked by one of the pastors of the church what I thought of Romania. I do not now remember my response, but recall the pastor turning to the SGA teacher and commenting, 'He's caught, you know!' There is no doubt that this was true.

In 2005 I had opportunity to visit the Emanuel Baptist University in Oradea to deliver a lecture to the students. The end result was a request to join the staff in the role of adjunct Professor. I was assured that this would make it possible to introduce Masters Studies into the University. Brother Gigi, Pastor of the Baptist Church in Medias and NT teacher in Emanuel jokingly said, 'Don't die, otherwise the University will lose their recognition!' So from 2005, year by year I became involved in the Masters' weeks of teaching, in addition to my teaching responsibilities in IBC and in Castlereagh. Today many more pastors and Emanuel graduates have been able to pursue studies to a higher level and to deepen their whole understanding of the word of God through the permission given for Masters' research.

The Comfort of Psalm 16
My wife Eileen had been feeling unwell for some time. I was in Romania teaching for SGA (2 weeks) when the Hospital concerns were expressed. The doctor said, 'I will have confirmation in one week, but I can tell you now…' this was the disturbing initial diagnosis. We discussed if I should come home right away – I was entering the second week of teaching in a different location.

Her commitment to me and the work remained unchanged, insisting that as it would be a week until we would be sure, I should stay. When I reached home the diagnosis of cancer was confirmed followed by the waiting time for treatment. Those were difficult days, but there was a well of support from many people. We discussed everything, accepting that we were all subject to sickness through the Fall of Adam and Eve. The question should not be 'Why me?' but 'Why not me?' She was able to accept the situation with such serenity. On one occasion as a male nurse called to give her the daily injection she commented to him, 'I cannot lose. If you can help me, I will be with my family; if not, I will be with my Lord'.

Surgery was performed Christmas week 2005. They almost lost her during the operation. The recovery began followed by radiotherapy treatment. The support of the local Macmillan nurses was second to none. I was able to work in IBC for a couple of days a week, with my youngest daughter Pamela (still living at home) taking time off to cover the other days. But the disease could not be stopped. On Monday 9th April 2007, after three days in the Marie Curie Hospital, Kensington Road, Belfast, with all our family in attendance, she slipped peacefully into the presence of the Lord. Pastor Roy McMullan, who had undertaken to visit regularly during the months of illness and to provide pastoral care for us as a family and Pastor Val English, a friend from 1967, shared in the funeral services in the home and in Castlereagh Baptist.

Eileen had proved to be a faithful and loving wife during our 39 years of marriage, a total support in every situation. When things were tight financially she was ready to take on full time employment both in Magherafelt and then later in Belfast. Since we had served in different churches, plus my college involvement, there were many in attendance at the funeral. The most important part of the funeral service was the message by Val on Psalm 16, particularly the assurances of v10-11. 'For thou wilt not leave my soul in hell: neither wilt thou suffer thine Holy One to see corruption. Thou wilt show me the path of life: *in thy presence is fullness of joy; at thy right hand there are pleasures for evermore*'. She would not want to come back from such fulfilment. Now she had perfect healing (Psalm 103v3, 'Who forgiveth all thine iniquities; who healeth all thy diseases'. I had read with her in the Marie Curie ward when she could no longer respond, the precious assurances of Hebrews

12v22-23. We are 'come unto Mount Sion, and unto the city of the living God, the heavenly Jerusalem, and to an innumerable company of angels, To the general assembly and church of the firstborn, which are written in heaven, and to God the judge of all, and *to the spirits of just men made perfect'*. She was going to be with her sister Evelyn, who also went home to be with the Lord in January after only a few weeks of illness (the two sisters had been in the hospital together at the one time!) and was with all the others who await their glorious resurrection when Christ returns. Eileen's death/victory day was actually Easter Monday that particular year, which brought the comfort that on that day Christ arose as the firstfruits – giving us the assurance that 'afterward they that are Christ's at his coming', (1 Cor. 15v23).

When bereavement comes people can go through a full range of emotions, but for me the strongest was guilt. I loved my wife and I felt that we had not had enough time together – just for us. If we had reached retirement perhaps you say to yourself things would have been different…But she had never complained about the work load I carried. I must leave my life as I lived it for God to decide. One note of joy in her home call for us was the salvation of one of her work colleagues. D had worked with Eileen for a couple of years. When she rang to ask how she was, Eileen would witness to her reminding her of the uncertainty of life; she would always procrastinate. But God was at work in her heart. 'I need to do something about this', she told her husband. She noticed that Rev. Sammy Workman was holding a mission near where she lived and determined to go. After the message she said to her husband 'I must talk to this man', and that night she trusted the Lord! 'I must phone Eileen', she said. But Eileen had just gone home to be with the Lord. So she came to tell us instead. God had honoured Eileen's witness.

Gideon's Fleece
I had stepped back from preaching in Castlereagh to care more for Eileen in the months before her home call. In September 2006, following fourteen years of my ministry, the church inducted Keith Giles as Pastor. Now I threw myself into my work at the College in the weeks and months that followed. I still had three years until retirement. I also had opportunity to return again to Romania from 18th-29th October. We began first in the SGA School in

Bicske, in Hungary for three days and then went on into Romania, to Zalau and Oradea. I recall my experience that first night in Bicske. I was staying in a little room in the huge church building. The alarm had been set downstairs so I could not get out. I woke in the night with the feeling that I was so alone. I remembered the first time I had come out with the SGA teacher who had to get home. Should I not do the same rather than going on into Romania for the whole trip? Then the Lord reminded me of an old Hymn.

> 'Thy life was given for me; thy blood O Lord was shed,
> that I might ransomed be, and quickened from the dead.
> Thy life was given for me; what have I given for thee?'
> The next verse reads:
> 'Long years were spent for me, in weariness and woe,
> that through eternity thy glory I might know.
> Long years were spent for me; have I spent one for thee?'
> Then the crucial verse:
> 'The father's home of light, the rainbow circled throne,
> were left for earthly night, for wanderings sad and lone.
> Yea, all was left for me; have I left aught for thee?'

The Lord reminded me that he had left the glory and splendour of heaven for earthly wanderings; he was really alone even if he had his disciples. He had spent not a few weeks but thirty three years on earth for me! Could I not spend a couple of weeks for him? God renewed my spirit and commitment. My sacrifice was nothing compared to his.

More and more God placed Romania on my heart. I remember when Cristi Galatanu, sent and supported by Rev Norman Fox of Norman Fox Missionary Cause, came to begin his College studies. At Morning Prayers, early in his first year he recounted the day he pointed an old man in a village to Christ. The man was so full of joy in his salvation. He said to Cristi, 'Are there many others who know about this salvation?' He explained that there were others, a church of people back in the city of Iasi. Then came the heart rending comments, 'My father needed to know this; and my grandfather. Why have you been so long in coming to tell us?'

There are 23 million Romanians who need the gospel. Only 4% of the country is evangelical! There are still 8,000 villages without a gospel witness of any kind. My heart was burdened, broken at such a great need. Romania was always in my mind. But how is one brought to the point of decision in making a commitment to go? I remember one morning before leaving for work. As my normal practice I spent time reading the bible – letting God speak to me and I to him. That morning I prayed earnestly, 'Lord, if you really want me to go you need to show me. When I go into IBC in Moira today let someone speak to me about Romania'. Then I thought that such a thing may just happen for no real reason. So I prayed again, 'Lord let someone mention Romania every day for three days. Then I will know'. It happened just like that! The first morning there were some people in the College to be interviewed as prospective students. At the coffee break, one of them spoke to me about Romania four times. I recall thinking, this is really serious. The next day, the same thing happened at the lunch table. And the third day? I normally took another lecturer with me to College, Dr. Maurice Dowling. Before we had gone any further than the carriageway, he opened up a discussion about Romania. What was I now going to do? God had me in a corner; I must go otherwise I would be disobedient to the Lord. He had revealed his will.

Of course, care and wisdom are required, as I stated earlier in the book, in seeking to discern the guidance of God. God has given us at least thirty thousand promises in his word. It is true that they are the promises of the God who 'cannot lie', Tit. 1v2. But we must remember that some are 'if' promises – there are conditions attached; some are given specifically to individuals or nations (e.g., the promise of God giving the land of Canaan to Abraham or the nation of Israel); some will be general promises for the whole Church e.g., the promise of his return. Yet there are promises for individuals. Here we need to take care in claiming the guidance of God for us. Many statements will be a specific promise made in special circumstances to a specific individual. It is true that God by his Spirit can sometimes give us a sense that he is applying them to us. But one will look also for other factors to accompany this sense; an inner burden or conviction that one should take a particular direction; circumstances; the advice of friends, 'in the multitude of counsellors there is safety', (Prov. 11v14). These will often come together to help us discern the will of God. However let us never rule out also the possibility of God acting in a dramatic way in response to prayer as in the matter of the fleece mentioned above, when I was left with no other choice than to go.

But the point was when would I be able to go? I had commitments to fulfil. Of course the time was getting closer for me to step back from the role as Principal. I knew that soon the discussion was to begin to search for my replacement. When I learned that a Committee was meeting to set down some guidelines as to the way to proceed I wrote to them through the Chairman, the Association Director, Billy Colville. I explained my commitment to Romania for the future and offered to leave one year earlier to get out into the work there. They were uneasy about this idea. The constituency would get the wrong message. If I went earlier like this it would be assumed either that I was unhappy with the Committee's handling of the matter or that the Committee had pushed me out a year before I was to go. No, I must let things continue until the normal time when the College would have opportunity to acknowledge my twenty years of service properly. But they suggested that if I could organise cover for my lectures for the first semester, from September to December, then come back for the second semester, that would be acceptable. So God opened up a way for me to get to Romania from September 2009. I returned for the final few months from February to June 2010. It was a joy to hand over my ministry in the College to Pastor Edwin Ewart (appointed Principal), who I had known first as a boy in Magherafelt in my first term there and as a student in IBC during my second. Also to see the appointment of Dr. Peter Firth as Biblical Studies Tutor, whom I had supervised through his PhD studies.

I thank God for all the ways he led me from those early days. The correspondence work with GCSEs and A level studies; the years in the Irish Baptist College, the postgraduate work through my final years in Glenarm and Magherafelt. The teaching I have done and continue to do in Emanuel University would not have been possible without all this. The pieces of the jigsaw fit.

Developments at IBC

I thank God for giving me the opportunity to serve in IBC at a crucial moment – 'for such a time as this'. In the early days among Irish Baptists, as I perceive among other groupings, to have acquired a BD degree was the pinnacle of achievement. Gradually things had been changing with Dr. Oakley taking his Masters and then his own PhD. When I enrolled in Postgraduate research, the Masters and particularly the PhD, there was no-one in IBC who could take on NT supervision. Now of course in secular education university students generally will not stop at the primary degree; they will need a Masters at least, and in fact most do continue to Doctoral studies. So it was important because of the higher level of education to have – as indicated the 'pieces of the jigsaw' in place. During the nineties and through into the 21st century, supervision to this level was required and also because of the changes in society there was an urgent need for a College course that would provide a much more practical element of preparation.

Two changes should be noted concerning the College in those days which meant that it was better at providing for the needs of all. First, the College moved from Belfast to Moira. The days of the property boom meant that the Baptist Union offices on Lisburn Road, plus the College building on Sandown Road could be sold for an excellent price. A site outside Moira was found for a 'Baptist Centre' which could accommodate both Office and College. Some took time to be persuaded of the move. But over the years it has proved to be an excellent location, what with the intersection of roads, the A1 to the South, the M1 to the West and to Belfast and the Airport Road heading north. The second change was in the nature of the courses available. The first step was having a course which included practical elements of ministry preparation and experience. We organised a Committee comprised of College Board, Association and Mission personnel, tasked to put together an ideal course for students – hence the adoption of the 'Preparation for Ministry' course, with its emphasis on practical training.

A further change in the courses took place at postgraduate level. We saw that it was vital also to provide a way for individuals already in ministry or mission to fulfil either their aspirations for further study, or the requirements for missionary involvement overseas. Our constant frustration had been to meet the entry requirements of Queen's University for Masters and PhD study. I recall travelling first with John Birnie (Secretary of the College at the time) all the way from the airport in Cardiff to the University of Lampeter. Later we formed a relationship with Chester University. The link with these universities opened up new possibilities for postgraduate study for so many mature students, who were without the normal entrance requirements.

At one point we had an amazing number of Postgraduate students which assisted the College financially but added greatly to our workload. For a small staff it was demanding both in supervision and in the administration of the courses. Yet it brought a great sense of fulfilment and joy to see people succeed, gain in confidence especially with their latent abilities and go out to be used of God in a more effective ministry. The College was endeavouring to provide for the needs of the churches and seeking to effectively prepare students at every level. I could leave with a sense of satisfaction that I had helped in some small way to prepare others to further the kingdom of God. But there was another 'army' to be influenced and taught in Emanuel University, Oradea.

My mother and father

Why am I sitting here?

DR HAMILTON MOORE: EVANGELIST PASTOR PRINCIPAL MISSIONARY

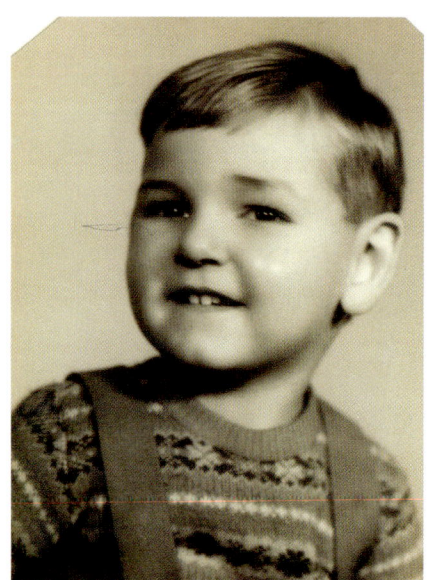

School Days

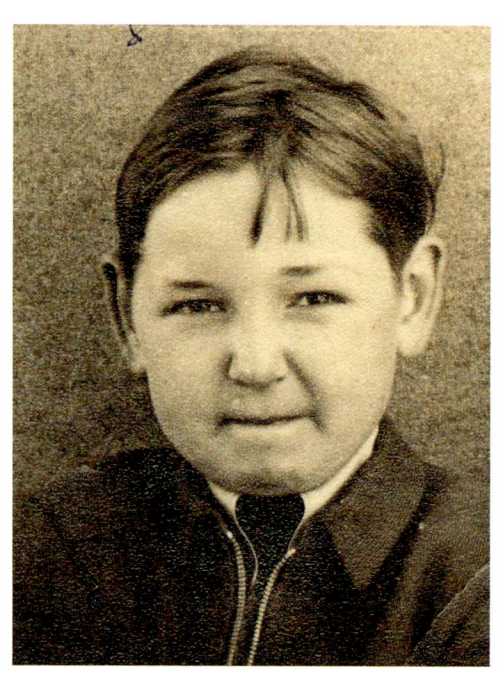

Photo Section

My son

Mum and sister shopping

Just a simple word of greeting,
Just a kindly thought to-day;
May your life be fair and happy,
May the sun shine on your way.

CHRISTMAS, 1921.

With Hearty Greetings
and Best Wishes
not only for Christmas
but for all time.

From
Jean Wilkinson

36 Candahar Street,
Belfast.

My wife Eileen and I with our children Wendy, David and Pamela

NEWSCENE

GLENARM
New Premises Opened

A crowd of almost two hundred people attended the opening of the new premises of the Glenarm Baptist Church on Saturday 27th July.

The opening ceremony was conducted by Pastor H. Moore B.D. (Magherafelt) and the building was declared open to the glory of God by one of the senior members of the church, Mr. N. Houston. Pastor J. R. Grant (B.U.O.I. secretary) was the chairman for the opening service and the Union President, Mr. S. N. Hamilton, read the scriptures and prayed.

A brief history of the building, which dated back to the eighteenth century and has served as the local courthouse, and a history of the Baptist witness in Glenarm were brought by Leslie Morrow (church secretary). Pastor S. Carson (Banbridge) was the speaker and musical items were provided by Larne Gospel Singers and Mr. Jackie McIlwaine. The vote thanks was given by Mr. T. Wright and greetings were brought by Pastor H. Moore, Mr. Trevor Boyd, Mr. S. Hamilton, Pastor Ken Humphries (Monkstown) and Alderman T. D. Robinson, Mayor of Larne.

The Benediction was pronounced by Mr. Billy Kernohan and tea, provided by the ladies, ended the afternoon.

Mr. S. Hamilton was the speaker at the services the next day and Pastor S. Carson commenced a two week mission on Monday 29th July.

Fourth from left, Bobby McClements, next to my father

Evangelical Youth Movement Team. Second left, Ed Adams, Director, next to myself

Photo Section

Irish Baptist College, Sandown Road, Belfast

People's Hall, Portavogie

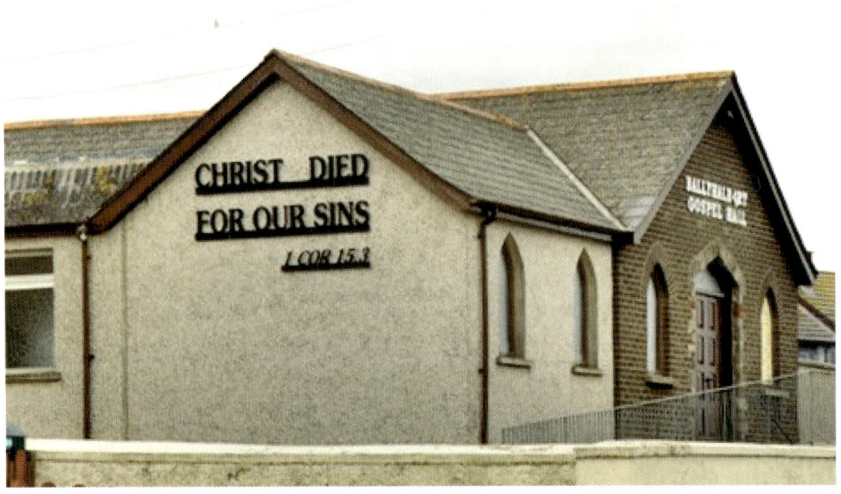

Ballyhalbert Gospel Hall

Photo Section

Templemore Hall, Belfast

Aughrim Gospel Hall, South Derry

Desertmartin Union Hall

Glenarm Baptist Church

First Queen's University, Belfast. Graduation, 1983

Emanuel Chapel Window (The Sower)

Emanuel University

Special night of blessing. Sixteen people respond to the gospel

DR HAMILTON MOORE: EVANGELIST PASTOR PRINCIPAL MISSIONARY

Emanuel University Graduation 2015

Graduation of Romanian Pastors in Cluj, University of Wales Masters Degree (IBC)

The first fruits of Odoreu for Christ

The Church in Odoreu today with Emanuel students

PART TWO: HAMILTON MOORE –
Missionary; Adjunct Professor; Founder of Tell Romania

(A) Hamilton Moore – Missionary in Romania – Land of Pain and the Power of God

I MUST CONFESS that I knew very little about Romania until the few students I mentioned in Part One were accepted in IBC. Naturally, I had heard of the fall of communism and Ceausescu, but everything seemed so remote from the ministry upon which I was constantly focused. Never did I foresee that I would travel there or that it would come to form such a huge part of my life. I have outlined my call to that needy land while I was Principal of IBC; now I must focus upon the land of Romania itself – a land of terrible suffering and yet a country where the power of God continues to work and transform lives.

The Bread Basket of Europe
Over the past number of years I have learned a lot about the country, its geographical location but also its past suffering under fascism and communism, plus the blessing that the gospel brought and continues to bring. Romania is situated in the South-eastern part of Central Europe and shares borders with Hungary and Serbia to the West, Bulgaria to the South, the Black Sea to the East. Ukraine and the Republic of Moldova lie mainly North and Northeast. It is the twelfth largest country in Europe. One third of the country consists of the Carpathian Mountains (also known as the Transylvanian Alps), extending over six hundred miles. Another third is hills and plateaus, with orchards and vineyards. The final third is a fertile plain, largely available for agriculture. The Danube River ends its journey of almost

1864 miles through Europe in South-eastern Romania.[25] Romania was once considered 'the bread basket of Europe'.[26] This was so during the time of the Ottoman Empire and later in the 1930s Romania was one of the main European producers of wheat and corn. But the situation was to change when in the 1950s the main communist leader of Romania, next to Ceausescu, Gheorghe Gheorghiu Dej, began developing heavy industry. The rich, fertile farmlands were abandoned through a policy of intensive industrialization as farmers were put under pressure to abandon their land and move to the cities. But we need to sketch the earlier history. We begin our quick survey from the time of the Second World War.

The Ethnic Germans in Romania
As you drive through various towns and villages in Romania one is quickly made aware of the significant German (Saxon) heritage in its beautiful buildings and architecture. In the past Germans were a sizeable minority population. Some resided in the centre of the country, in places like Sibiu, Brasov and Sighisoara, others in the West e.g., Timisoara. Also there was a sparsely populated area between Romania and a small piece of southern Ukraine called Bessarabia.[27] This area became part of Romania in 1918, with the inhabitants retaining their German heritage while being loyal Romanian citizens. So at the beginning of World War II there were around 800,000 Germans living in Romania. Not for long, however.

In 1940, Bessarabia and northern Bukovina were occupied by Soviet troops and it was agreed with Hitler to resettle more than 93,000 Bessarabian Germans to the Reich.[28] They were allowed to take food and whatever personal property they could carry, but there was no compensation for their homes, businesses or wealth. They ended up primarily in camps in Saxony, Bavaria, the Sudetenland, Austria and West Prussia. In January 1945, Russian troops advanced on these regions, and the Germans suffered tremendous losses while trying to flee. Many were deported to the Caucasus and to Siberia. Again, at the end of the war, the Soviets ordered the expulsion of Germans from Romania early in 1945. Their deportation for forced labour was the Soviet idea of 'German war reparations' according to the 1944 secret Soviet Order 7161 issued to the last non-communist government of Romania under Nicolae Radescu. It is estimated that around 75,000 to 100,000 Transylvanian Germans were deported, including the newly installed President, Iohannis' grandparents.[29]

During the 1950s, there was more grim hardship to come upon Romania's ethnic Germans as the Romanian Communist government began a large-scale action of penal transportation. Their aim was to forcibly relocate individuals who lived within approximately twenty five km of the Yugoslav border so as to 'purify' the whole region. During the night of June 18, 1951, 45,000 people were taken from their homes at gunpoint, herded on to wagons under military guard and deported to the Baragan area, an underdeveloped, sparsely populated area in South-east Romania. They suffered two weeks of gruelling travel, and were then dumped there and left to build houses of mud and straw in eighteen localities. Finally, what has been described as the greatest slave trade in European history happened later as the dictator Ceausescu devised a policy of 'selling' ethnic Germans in Romania who wished to leave Romania, to the Bonn Government. They were 'sold' for 8,000 to 14,000 Deutsche Marks each, making a total 'profit' of about 500 million Euros, a slave trade which ended only when Ceausescu was executed.[30] But what of the Jews?

The Romanian Jews

At one time there were said to be around sixty synagogues in Oradea. Today, there are two. I recall going with two students from Emanuel to see part of the city of Oradea. We were able to visit the area where there is a courtyard with a memorial to the Holocaust victims. The synagogue was nearby. Until recently, the building displayed the bullet holes which were reminders of the Nazi oppression against those who had tried to find shelter there. It was sobering to stand outside the synagogue and try to visualise what it must have meant for the Jewish families who sought refuge there without success.

When the second World War broke out, Romania under King Carol II adopted, officially at first, a position of neutrality. But many factors were to change this in 1940. These included the fall of France; territorial losses involving a Soviet ultimatum; and locally, in Romania, the rise of the Iron Guard, urging an alliance with Nazi Germany. The government's popularity was low and the resultant coup led to the setting up of a fascist dictatorship under General Ion Antonescu. Romania proceeded to commit more troops to the Eastern Front than all of Germany's other allies. Later, as the fortunes of war turned against Germany, Romania was bombed in 1943 by the Allies and invaded by Soviet troops in 1944. Romania switched sides and Prince Michael led a successful coup deposing the Antonescu regime.[31] One can state that Jewish anti-Semitism reached a horrific all-time high during the alliance with Germany.

It appears to be still a difficult subject to discuss and to establish facts concerning this 'dark period'. The fact is clear that once in power in October 1940 the Iron Guard commenced a serious Anti-Semitic campaign. It is claimed that in Romania's or shall we say Antonescu's alliance with Nazism, in the early years of the war, horrific events happened in places such as Bucharest and Iasi but also in Transnistria and Odessa. These final two areas were part of Romania at that time but are no longer so when borders were redrawn at the end of the war. It is estimated that between 280,000 and 380,000 Jews died.[32]

Following the war the Romanian People's Tribunals were held to bring to account those who so brutally had carried out or were responsible for the deaths of so many Jews. The record[33] states:

> The Bucharest Tribunal sentenced a total of 187 people. At the main trial, in May 1946, of the leaders of the former Fascist government of Ion Antonescu, twenty four defendants stood before the Tribunal. The court handed down 13 death sentences, but six were pronounced in absentia and never carried out. Of the remaining seven death sentences, 3 were commuted to life imprisonment. Ion Antonescu, Mihai Antonescu, Constantin Vasiliu and Gheorghe Alexianu were executed on June 1, 1946 at Jilava prison. The other defendants were sentenced to life imprisonment, or long terms of imprisonment. The Cluj Tribunal ... sentenced 481 people: 370 were Hungarian, 83 were German, 26 were Romanian and 2 were Jewish. The Cluj Tribunal passed a total of 100 death sentences, 163 sentences of life imprisonment, and a range of other sentences.

The report commissioned and accepted by the Romanian government in 2004 on the Holocaust concluded:

Of all the allies of Nazi Germany, Romania bears responsibility for the deaths of more Jews than any country other than Germany itself. The murders committed in Iasi, Odessa, Bogdanovka, Domanovka, and Peciora, for example, were among the most hideous murders committed against Jews anywhere during the Holocaust. Romania committed genocide against the Jews. The survival of Jews in some parts of the country does not alter this reality.[34]

But to return to the Jewish community in Oradea, the city which has special significance for me and for this account of my life, as we are based in Emanuel University. The city was under Nazi rule and Hungarian control because of the acceding of Northern Transylvania to Hungary in the Second Vienna Award[35] of 1940.[36] During the first part of the war there were about 25,000 Jews living there. In 1944 the Hungarian authorities forced the Jewish inhabitants into the Oradea ghetto before sending the majority of them to the Auschwitz concentration camp. The few that did remain were 'freed' by the westward march of the Soviet army. Unfortunately, their fate was not much better under Soviet rule than it had been under the brief reign of the Nazis and the Hungarians. Though they were not sent to concentration camps, the Soviets simply marched them into the streets and shot them. For the Jews who still remain in Oradea, I continue to take New Testaments in Hebrew from the Society for Distributing Hebrew Scriptures and give them to the students in Emanuel to share with their Jewish friends.

The Roma Communities
What of the Roma people? Historians tell us that Roma origins lie in Northwest India and their migration towards Europe began from the 3rd to the 7th century AD. The Roma were among the first victims of the Nazi policies of racial and biological purity. They were sent to Chelmno to the gas vans for extermination. In the camps, they were subjected to gruesome experiments. Around 500,000 Roma people were exterminated under fascist rule. Estimates vary concerning present numbers.[37] Roma people make up around 3.6% to 4.3% of the population[38] in Romania, being the second-largest ethnic minority after Hungarians. Most Roma families live in small shacks on the edge of villages, with no running water and often no electricity. International agencies estimate that poverty among them is generally ten times higher than in the

local population where they live, and their lifespan is ten to fifteen years shorter. Yet God has worked among them in great blessing – the power of God, in spite of the pain – as I will now share.

Revival among the Roma
Pata Rat[39] is located on the edge of the city of Cluj Napoca, in the heart of Transylvania and covers 18 hectares. It is the home of three distinct groups of Roma people that live in two districts, ironically named "Dallas I", "Dallas II" and a third one that lives up on the Pata Rat landfill, a total of around 1,500 people. Most live in poor dwellings, 2 metres high, 4 metres wide, cottages made of recovered materials, covered in bitumen and plastic foil with no electricity nor sewage system. Here, they are in a sense providing a service for citizens of Cluj by collecting plastic bottles, metals, wood and everything that can be reused, repaired or recycled. The Baptist churches of Iris and Bethel reach out in love to this community by providing humanitarian aid. Our ministry, Tell Romania, has been able to send out to Cluj three 40 ft. lorries and part of the load has been the provision of clothes and others medical supplies to strengthen the hands of the teams who regularly visit the site and also share the gospel with those in such dire need. The grace and power of God is still changing lives.

In the past few years one pastor, Calin Talos, who was in the church in Peceiu in the Zalau area, used the Jesus film as a first step in evangelism. There was a mighty response – reminding me of the crowd who heard Peter preach on the day of Pentecost, 'Men and brethren, what shall we do?' The apostle did not leave it there but 'with many other words did he testify and exhort..'. (Acts 2v37-40). Eight churches were formed. In April 2015 I had opportunity to teach concerning the Cults for the SGA School in Pecieu and met some of the Roma men who attended, including Remus, a Bulibasa, or gypsy king. God had saved this man about ten years earlier and he had maintained a great testimony among his people. A Bulibasa will command great respect in a village and his involvement in the church will lead to acceptance by the community.

Calin asked me to consider coming back a couple of months later for a weekend only for the Roma men in one of their churches. Remus and his son, with around 30 men came for two nights and we were able to teach through

Paul's Epistle to the Romans, a precious time as the truths of the Gospel in that book were received with great joy and praise to God. They had grasped the wonder of what it means to be 'now' justified, (Romans 5v9)! What an experience to preach on four occasions on the Sunday, especially in Remus' church in the village of Huseni, where the people were hanging on to every word! SGA has now organised a special Mission School in one of their churches, Simleul-Silvaniei. Over forty students are now attending, packing into the small upper room. This is just one example of how God is moving powerfully among Roma people. In fact this is happening in many similar communities. We will now write about the Roma community in the village of Odoreu, two hours north of Oradea. God also moved in what we can only describe as revival. Not only is there a church planted among them and a building where they can worship the Lord, but they are now reaching out in evangelism to another group of needy Roma people. The pain of which we wrote had given way to the super abounding grace and power of God (Rom. 5v20).

Satu Mare and Odoreu
This opportunity for ministry among Roma people was in Satu Mare in Emanuel Baptist Church with brother Remus Oanta. Remus had organised an SGA School in his church in Satu Mare. I have had opportunity to teach on a number of occasions. On a particular Saturday a man called Joseph from the Roma people living in Odoreu attended. One needs to go back further to know the significance of this. A Roma community had been living in shacks on the riverbank in Satu Mare. Remus, with his wife Diana and some of the members of the Satu Mare church made contact with them, taking them some food and supplies. God no doubt was at work for they were received and accepted. Then the little community was moved on by the police but were found later living in hovels on the edge of the Odoreu village. Contact was renewed and the love shown to them opened their hearts. Joseph who had turned up at the School went on to be baptised with his wife Malinda. The baptisms took place during a Sunday morning service and many of the little community also came – no doubt moved by God and so seeking to understand what had happened to their friends. Back in Odoreu Joseph had a little 'house'

built of mud and straw with branches for a ceiling. He opened it for the people to come to hear the gospel and the numbers grew and grew. God was working in so many hearts. It was in 2010 that I found the firstfruits of Odoreu for Christ on a visit to Joseph's house.

It soon became clear that somewhere to meet was a priority. The house was full for the meetings, with people also having to stand outside at the windows. Another house nearby with a piece of ground was found. Plans were drawn up for a church building and they were accepted at the town hall. It was wonderful to see God turn up the necessary funds from various sources in NI, from my own ministry Tell Romania, various churches and individuals, from Christian Fellowship Trust and the ministry of Pastor David McFarland – enough to buy the land, pay the cost of getting the plans through and provide the necessary building materials. More important was the fact that Remus' two brothers were small contractors. But how could the church be built? People do not often realise the serious situation of the Roma families in Odoreu. They survive and put bread on the table for their families by what the men can find in the rubbish bins and at the Satu Mare dump! But now another way to get the money they needed was available. They came to learn how to build! Every morning at 7.00 am the men would stand outside the gate of the building site and in view of the whole street hold a prayer meeting before beginning the day's work. What a witness they were. They could earn enough for those weeks not to have to go to the bins. There was such a move of the Spirit at that time that many from the community would gather in the half built church building to hear the gospel being preached. What special days these were as we shared the Good News with people seeking to know the way of salvation, eager to hear the truth, anxious to know how God had changed the lives of other people and could also bring to them hope and assurance. By July 2012 the walls were up, the roof was fitted and the building was opened. A small plaque was unveiled to mark the event – a reminder of what God had done in Odoreu. The work has continued to be consolidated over the past few years. We continue to go back again and again to teach the church how to go on in their witness for the Lord, as Paul and Barnabas did in Acts 14v21-23, returning to Lystra, Iconium and Antioch, 'confirming the souls of the disciples, and exhorting them to continue in the faith'.

But our ministry also sought to witness to the Odoreu community through helping in practical ways. God enabled us to send a number of 45 ft. lorries filled with different items such as, clothes, beds, furniture, handbags filled with toiletries and 1,300 pairs of shoes (graciously gathered together by Newtownbreda Baptist Church). Following the building of the church, the local men have been able to erect a community hall and a boiler house – SGA have also helped them with radiators to help heat the main building. A stove brought from Larne heats the hall and Omagh Baptist Church provided money to get some heating stoves for individual houses.

But the people of the church are not just a community which is always taking from others, always looking for help. In little areas around the church building they have planted some vegetables and also built an oven made of breeze blocks where they bake bread. The real evidence of what God has done in their lives is the fact that they now are reaching out in love to others! Some Roma families were living under the stadium in Satu Mare. Contact was made and the little Christian community in Odoreu went into action, sharing some of the things they had received – clothes, shoe boxes of small items. They also provided the bread baked from their primitive breeze block oven situated outside the church for these destitute families. Their love and generosity did not of course stop at providing humanitarian aid – they were so keen to share the gospel, telling what God had done for them, in changing their lives. They talked one to one with those they had helped and even Sister Diana, the Pastor's wife took the opportunity to start teaching the children and young people gospel songs. Praise the Lord!

Orphanages and Orphans
Romania was called the 'land of the orphans', a reputation largely due to the legacy of its former ruthless dictator, Ceausescu and his wife and their pro-natalist policies. In his desire to build a large nation, Ceausescu wanted women to have at least five children which in reality they could not care for. Many women died in childbirth as a result of severe malnutrition and lack of medical care. Mothers gave birth to children they could not feed, giving them up to government orphanages which were estimated to house around 100,000 – 500,000 children.[40] In the years that followed 1989 there were thousands

of abandoned and orphaned children trying desperately to survive on the streets and in the sewers. Many of these street children died from starvation, disease and exposure to the brutal Romanian winters. Today even with an improving economy, Romania has around 80,000 orphaned or abandoned children in some sort of institutional care and an estimated three to five thousand homeless street children.[41] In September 2014 a decision was taken by the Romanian Government to prohibit the institutionalisation of children under three, in recognition of the extreme vulnerability of children aged 0-3 to the effects of institutional care.

The Caminul Felix Community and Casa Grace

God has also given me opportunity to be involved with orphan children in two ministries, Caminul Felix and Casa Grace. The first, Caminul Felix is a group of bungalows comprising two family villages just outside Oradea. The family concept is seen as the way to bring security and love to children who have been formally abandoned, abused and neglected, giving them time to heal and move forward into a new life. There are sixteen families with loving adoptive parents caring for over two hundred children. Some of the children are now making the transition into adulthood.

I was first introduced to these children when preaching in Sanmartin Baptist Church, close to Oradea. My translator was one of the parents, Mihai Bulc. First we visited his family and with the help of Omagh Baptist Church provided six new bunk beds for the children. Also at Christmas time Magherafelt Baptist Church sent out ninety-seven gifts, individually chosen for each boy or girl, according to age. A dental centre and dental equipment also was brought out on one of our lorries, plus some material for their 'Sunflower Room' – a little Cottage industry providing opportunity to learn dressmaking skills by those children who do not go on to university. Among Mihai's eleven children are four from one family – sadly their mother is serving a life sentence in prison for murder. How important is this ministry as the children now are brought up knowing the gospel and a saviour's love. The power of God overcomes the pain.

Casa Grace or Christian Agency for Social Action, which is a ministry of Emanuel Baptist Church, Oradea, carries on a similar work. I have been taking again and again some support to them when I have been there. The Agency[42] established in 1996 today incorporates three departments that work closely together to give the best care possible for those in the surrounding community. First, *Families in Difficulty* support approximately ninety families at any one time, within a sixty km radius of Oradea. These families receive little or no income. Families benefit from this programme with material and financial assistance, counselling, social and educational activities, parenting courses, and support groups. A *Vocational Training Centre* provides training in tailoring or computing for those with no formal qualifications, the unemployed, or those in need of additional training to keep their jobs. Each year over one hundred people graduate in tailoring and over two hundred graduate in the introductory European Computing Driving Licence (ECDL) course. Graduates are then either able to get a job, support themselves through their own business or help their family and community. *Kingdom Kids* works with orphans and poor children with special needs to improve their quality of life. This includes fulfilling their affection and emotional needs, and therapy to recover their motor and psychological deficiencies. God's love and grace is reaching out to those who need it so desperately in the land of Romania, the outcasts through poverty and illness. But we must also look back into Romania's dark past under communism and while we must remember the oppression of Christians under Ceausescu we must also recount the triumph of faith. It has been humbling to read of the suffering of the believers but challenging to record for you their victory.

Communism and Ceausescu
What of Romania after the war and under communism? The summary of the facts is as follows. As was noted above, in 1944 King Michael brought about a coup, with Romania changing sides and joining Soviet forces against fascist Germany. In 1945 the Yalta Agreement made Romania part of the Soviet system. But by 1947, with Soviet troops on its territory, the communists, who gradually took power, forced King Michael to abdicate and proclaim Romania a People's Republic. Gheorghe Gheorghiu-Dej became the communist leader of Romania from 1947 until his death in 1965. He was followed by Nicolae Ceausescu who had been a member of the Romanian Communist youth movement, and rose through the ranks of his predecessor's Socialist

government. Upon the death of Gheorghiu-Dej in 1965, he succeeded to the leadership of Romania's Communist Party as General Secretary.

Ceausescu rebuilt much of the capital city, Bucharest, destroying hundreds of historical buildings in the process. One of the most famous creations of his time is Casa Poporului (House of the People, now known as Parliament Palace) in Bucharest, the second largest building in the world, after the Pentagon. At one time, seventy percent of the GNP was used to build the Palace while the people starved. Ceausescu was obsessed with repaying to Western banks the national debt as soon as possible. To achieve this he ordered a ban on importation of any consumer products and commanded exportation of all goods produced in Romania except minimum food supplies. Huge queues would form in shops (many with empty shelves) as people would seek to buy the most basic things. Right after communism fell, Romania didn't have any external debt but had managed to pay it all off. However, in achieving this the dictator brought the country to poverty while his family had enjoyed unbridled luxury. He also developed the Securitate, the secret police that became a feared tool of repression. In December 1989, following the anti-communist revolt of the people, Ceausescu and his wife Elena were quickly judged by a military tribunal and executed.

Under communism many from the Orthodox, Greek Catholic, Lord's Army, Lutheran, Baptist, Pentecostal, and Christian Brethren suffered imprisonment. We are referring to thousands, not hundreds; the jails were full. The experience of one man will serve to illustrate the dreadful suffering, but also the triumph over evil, the power of God overcoming the pain.

Richard Wurmbrand (1909-2001)

Richard Wurmbrand was a Romanian Lutheran pastor of Jewish descent. A convinced atheist at first and unfaithful to his wife, but God brought him to a village high up in the mountains to an old carpenter who had prayed that before he was called home, since Jesus was Jewish, he would have the privilege of bringing a Jew to Christ. There were no Jews in the area but Wurmbrand was drawn irresistibly to *that* particular village out of the twelve thousand villages in Romania at the time, where he was given a bible and both he and his wife Sabina were converted! Wurmbrand was set on fire for God.

The Nazis came to power first. Wurmbrand[43] explains, 'We had much to suffer. In Rumania,[44] Nazism took the form of a dictatorship of extreme orthodox elements which persecuted Protestant groups as well as the Jews... My son Mihai had to be given a non-Jewish name to prevent his death'. On numerous occasions he and his wife were hauled before Nazi judges, threatened and beaten. Richard, having such a burden for those raised in atheism, began to witness to Russian prisoners. Then, as outlined earlier, one million Russian soldiers arrived in 1944; after them the communists came to power in the country. What happened under the Nazi terror was only a taste of what was to come under the communists.

Richard had two ministries. A public one as pastor of the Lutheran Mission and the representative of the World Council of Churches who were involved in relief work. But secretly he carried on a ministry among the Russian soldiers and a ministry to the underground church, those who were meeting in private homes, in the woods, in basements. Finally arrested in February 1948 and given the 'prison' name Vasile Georgescu so no one would ever trace him, he was held for fourteen years in various prisons in Romania; in Calea Rahova, Vacaresti, Tirgul–Ocna, the penal facilities of Craiova, Poarta-Alba, back to Vacaresti prison, then Jilava and ultimately Gherla.[45] In them all he experienced horrific beatings, torture, drugging, freezing in ice-box 'refrigerator cells' to within a minute or two of death, thawed out, then thrown back in again. He spent three years in solitary confinement, plus two years a patient in the 'death room' from which no-one is meant to leave alive. In 1950, his wife Sabine was also arrested and became a penal slave labourer for three years on the Danube canal. He was informed – in an attempt to add to his distress that she was dead and Mihai was in prison. He could write:

> We Christians were put in wooden boxes only slightly larger than we were. This left no room to move. Dozens of sharp nails were driven into every side of the box...We were forced to stand in these boxes for endless hours... When we became fatigued and swayed from tiredness...there were the horrible nails...What communists have done to Christians, surpasses any possibility of human understanding.[46]

In 1964 Christians in Norway secured his release, giving £2,500 to the communist government. He was to be the voice of the underground church to the Free World. In May 1966, when he came to America, Richard Wurmbrand testified before the American Senate's Internal Security Subcommittee. He took off his shirt and showed eighteen torture wounds covering his body. He could testify:

> I have seen Christians in communist prisons with 50 lbs. of chains on their feet, tortured with red-hot pokers, in whose throats spoonfuls of salt have been forced being kept after without water, starving, whipped, suffering from cold, and praying with fervour for the communists. This is humanly inexplicable! It is the love of Christ which was shed into their hearts.[47]

Solitary confinement involved being in a cell twelve feet underground, with no lights or windows. There is no sound because even the guards wore felt on the soles of their shoes. He later explained that he was able to maintain his sanity by sleeping during the day, staying awake at night, and focusing his mind and soul on constructing and then delivering a sermon each night. He had an extraordinary memory and was able afterwards to recall more than 350 of these, including a selection in his book *With God in Solitary Confinement*,[48] first published in 1969. During this time, he would communicate with other prisoners by tapping out the Scriptures in Morse code on the wall. In this way he continued to be pastor to others[49] and carried on as a constant witness of the good news of the gospel. He could write, 'Not just clergymen were put in prison, but also simple peasants, young boys and girls who witnessed for their faith. The prisons were full and in Rumania, as in all communist countries, to be in prison means to be tortured'.[50]

Imprisoned believers would be subjected to atheistic brainwashing. During his testimony before the US Congress Committee Wurmbrand[51] spoke not only about his own torture but the brainwashing he underwent in prison:

> Now the worst times came; the times of brain-washing. Those who have not passed through brain-washing can't understand what torture it is. From 5 in the morning until 10 in the evening... 17 hours a day... we had to sit just like this [he sat straight looking forward]. We were not allowed to lean. For nothing in the world could we rest a little bit-our head. To close your eyes was a crime! From 5 in the morning until 10 in the evening we had to sit like this and hear: "Communism is good. Communism is good. Communism is good. Communism is good. Communism is good. Christianity is stupid!

Christianity is stupid! Christianity is stupid! Nobody more believes in Christ. Nobody more believes in Christ. Give up! Give up! Give up!" For days, weeks, years, we had to listen to these things!

Yet amidst all the pain, physical and psychological, he experienced the power of God at work. In Calea Rahova he was interrogated by the young Lieutenant Grecu who had been indoctrinated with the conviction that what he was doing would make a better world. He would come to his desk with a rubber truncheon in his hand. Wurmbrand[52] recounts how Grecu demanded that he set down on paper the times he communicated in code with the others prisoners and also other breaches of prison rules. He was given thirty minutes. Richard had not written anything for so long, but in this 'declaration' he admitted he had broken rules, tapped the Gospel message through the walls, hoarded pills to kill himself, made a knife out of tin, and chessmen out of bread. Then he wrote, 'I have never spoken against the communists. I am a disciple of Christ, who has given us love for our enemies'.[53] Grecu returned exactly on time, still carrying his truncheon, with which he had been beating prisoners. Picking up the paper Grecu was so deeply challenged. How could Wurmbrand love someone who shut him away alone for years, beat him and starve him? They talked for two hours and for days they continued to meet. 'Two weeks later, in his khaki uniform with the blue tabs of the Security Police at his collar Grecu confessed to me in my patched prison rags. We became brethren'.[54]

Again, in Calea Rahova as he admitted to Grecu, Wurmbrand had communicated with other prisoners by means of a code. On one occasion he had learned to tap the wall using Morse code. The unknown prisoner on the other side of the wall was a radio engineer on a capital charge. They became 'Morse' friends and communicated about many things, the Scriptures, the man's spiritual state and more mundane matters – until the guard discovered what was happening. Wurmbrand was moved to another cell. In time many of the prisoners learned the code. Years later in Jilava in a cell which had one hundred men crushed into it (some suffocated to death there) he sat down on a bunk with another man to eat his rotten carrot soup. The man had sent information to a patriotic group in the west and mentioned he had been brought to Christ through his knowledge of Morse code. 'In the cells of the Ministry of Interior...an unknown pastor tapped Bible verses to me through the wall'. Wumbrand replied, 'I was that pastor'.[55] The power of the Scriptures, the power of God overcame. Even Gheorghiu Dej, Romania's communist leader from 1947 to 1965, confessed his faith and died a converted man.

The triumph of the Church in the communist oppression was evidenced in its poetry and hymnology. There are songs still sung today which were composed then – although sadly sometimes the circumstances of the composition is forgotten. One example of such hymn writers was Nicolae Moldoveanu. He was arrested in 1959 and sentenced to twelve years in prison. Wurmbrand met him in Gherla and his commendation reveals again the power of God at work at the time:

> The first person I saw was my former cell-mate Nicolaie Moldovanu from the Army of the Lord, a Romanian version of the Salvation Army, but without uniforms and bands. We had been in the same cell in the ancient prison in Gherla. The regime had been very harsh. From time to time, wardens would shout, "Everyone on the ground!" It was winter. We had no sweaters, let alone overcoats. The floor was cold concrete with not even a bit of straw for warmth. Prisoners cursed the brutality of the wardens. Not so Moldovanu. He believed that praising God was better than cursing Communists. With a beautiful smile on his lips, he would say, "Let's forget our surroundings. I'll sing you the song I just composed while lying on my stomach." It was a hymn full of joy, hope and praise, sung now in many countries.[56]

Revival in Oradea

One must also narrate the power of God at work in Oradea, the revival blessing which began in Emanuel Baptist Church, spread throughout the country and led to the establishment of Emanuel Christian University. These events will reveal the opposition and subtlety of the communist authorities; but also reveal how pastors remained faithful and how some could be 'compromised'.

The roots of Emanuel University[57] were planted in 1970s, when Emanuel Baptist Church of Oradea, formerly known as the Second Baptist Church of Oradea, initiated an underground Bible 'school' to train the future pastors and missionaries of Communist Romania. Romanians love to visit the forests for holidays in the summer. It is almost part of their culture, because for many years under communism they had no opportunity of travelling outside Romania. So the men would take their families to the forest. But some were not really there to have a vacation but to study the word. A teacher – often from BEE (Bible Education by Extension)[58] or SGA would also secretly be among them. The men would be packed together into the roof space of the place where they were staying in a searing heat, while the women and children played nearby. Should the Securitate appear the men would quickly descend and everything would be as normal – families simply enjoying a summer holiday. John Birnie, Director of Field Ministries, SGA (UK) has written a book on the Rector of Emanuel Baptist University, Oradea, Romania, Paul Negrut. In *Just Call me Paul,* he reveals that while there was a Baptist Seminary in Bucharest the authorities permitted only between three to five students to enrol for theological training every two years. Sadly the training was severely controlled and regulated. 'These severe limits on training for ministry were designed to keep the churches weak and ineffective. The Communist authorities were following a well-known and proven strategy, this is, confine and control the leadership, and so control the whole movement'.[59] However, by the mid 1980s, not just study in the forest, but a 'School of the Prophets' was operating secretly in the annex of the Second Baptist Church! It was really the revival in the Second Baptist and the fall of Ceausescu in 1989 which led to the establishment of Emanuel Baptist University. The man that God used was first of all Liviu Olah.

Liviu Olah

Liviu Olah[60] first graduated from the Faculty of Law in Bucharest. He was a member of the Baptist Church located at Odobescu in Timisoara, working for God, especially with young people. Liviu was a man of prayer calling the church to return to the practice of prayer and fasting like the Christian church of the first century. In 1968 he was finally ordained as pastor of the first Baptist Church in Timisoara where ninety new members were added to the existing ones – ignoring the requirements of the authorities for approval of baptisms. In 1973 he accepted the invitation to serve as pastor of the Second Baptist Church of Oradea. Nikolai Covaciu was then pastor of the church and president of the Baptist Denomination. He had suffered a heart attack and was still unwell, so insisted the authorities accept Liviu Olah as the assistant pastor of the church. Birnie[61] comments concerning this man Covaciu, 'Throughout his lengthy pastorate and his role as Baptist Union President, he had been working hand in hand with the secret police. He was compromised spiritually, practically and politically, and in large measure was responsible for the lamentable state of Oradea's 2nd Baptist's church life'. The authorities would have agreed to this appointment simply because they were sure of Covaciu's co-operation and his ability to control the situation, or so they thought.

As soon as Olah began preaching he called the church to repentance, to abandon their 'lukewarm' Christianity, to forsake drunkenness – a particular problem at the time – and commit themselves to earnest prayer, Bible reading, and personal evangelism. God worked in many hearts and moved by his Spirit many, many people confessed their sin. The largest baptism in the history of Baptists in Romania dates back to this time when one hundred and forty nine people professed faith in Jesus Christ. The church and the courtyard were crowded to capacity to hear the word. Revival had come to Oradea and spread out through the whole region as others (choirs and preachers from the church) went out Sunday by Sunday to tell of what God was doing and how their lives had been transformed. After the fall of communism the present church building was erected to seat over three thousand people. In fact there are over four thousand members although the difficulties in providing for their families has resulted, as in other parts of Romania, in members of the church having to live and work outside the country.

We noted that the idea of establishing a Christian university was born in this time of awakening under Liviu Olah. All this became a reality after 1989 with the fall of communism. The power of God overcame the oppression and the pain. In 1990, the Church founded the Emanuel Theological School, from the 'School of the Prophets', ultimately reorganized as a university. The desire to respond to the needs of the country when Ceausescu fell led to the vision to prepare young people to make a difference in the country by offering study programs, along with theology, in the areas of philology, social sciences, music and management. These young people would not only be formally equipped for their different professions, but through study of the Scriptures were being sent as salt and light wherever they would go.

Since its establishment, Emanuel University still operates under the spiritual authority of Emanuel Baptist Church in Oradea, headed by the pastors, Peter Vidu, Dorin Hnatiuc, Paul Negru and Cosmin Marc. Brother Paul is the Rector. Currently, Emanuel University in Oradea is the only accredited conservative Baptist University in Europe. The stained glass window in the chapel at Emanuel University depicts the sower sowing the seed of the word of God is a reminder to all in Emanuel of the aim of the university, i.e., that every graduate will take the Gospel with them into the market place, into the towns and villages of Romania and throughout the world.

Paul Negrut

When Pastor Olah left in 1977 he was replaced by Iosif Ton who remained as pastor until 1981. Two men, Nick Gheorghita, a medical doctor and well-known preacher and brother Paul Negrut, a clinical psychologist, were elected to the pastorate of the church in 1982. Paul's experiences also make clear the serious oppression from the State and yet how God's power was at work. Birnie[62] includes in his biography of Paul, the Rector's insights into the subtlety of the communists in their attempts to bring pastors under their influence until they become informers and agents of the state:

> In the wake of the 2nd World War many church buildings had been damaged and destroyed…Into this 'hopeless' situation came representatives of the state to offer help to repair and rebuild…Many were deceived, naively believing that the communist authorities were their helpers and protectors and failing to see that the motivation was to control, limit, and eventually destroy the ministry of the Gospel. They did not see that 'communism' was not merely a particular form of government, but an ideology, an all-embracing world which was in essential and fundamental opposition to the faith of the Bible…Sadly, pastors too were deceived, even to the point that many became agents of the state, informing on those who resisted and refused to be brought under state control.

Like Richard Wurmbrand and others, Paul refused to ever allow such control. Being in a leadership position in the church placed a man and his wife and family under great stress – one never knew when the house could be raided or going out if the father would ever return. The aim was to instil a high level of anxiety day after day. In Paul's experience, in 1988, on Christmas eve, an attempt was made to electrocute him and his family. All the pipes became 'live'. In the attic a line connecting the mains electric from a street pole to the drainage system of the house was discovered. God preserved his servant and some young people who were visiting in his home at the time and so the work of God continued in the church and to this day. This was just one example of the constant pressure and the danger which he and his family were constantly subjected to.

In all such experiences Paul was protected and upheld by God. He would not compromise as others have done. In light of his courage and stand against the communist oppression, the late Margaret Thatcher, who was British Prime Minister at the time, awarded him the Torch of Freedom in 1990; in 2000 he was made a 'Knight of the Order of Faithful Service' by the Romanian President himself, in recognition of his support for freedom of conscience and religion in Romania and his opposition to religious repression. So while some men sadly compromised and caved in under the pressure from the Secret Police, Paul Negrut stood firm and was mightily used in the days of revival blessing in Oradea and in the country of Romania. During the days when he was a young man in Oradea, in the 2nd Baptist Church; as part of the group who secretly studied the Scriptures; in his role as pastor of the church; in the uncertainty of family life from which he could have been taken away at any time, God's power caused him to triumph through all the persecution and unceasing pressure from the authorities.

John Birnie[63] recounts that in the summer of 1989 Ceausescu came to Oradea and one of his stopping places was outside the building where the 2nd Baptist Church met. He was well acquainted with the situation as the names of Paul Negrut and Nick Gheorghita had been mentioned on many reports of the Secret Police in Bucharest, plus the unwavering support of the church members for their pastors. He issued what was really an order to the local Securitate, 'When I come back to Oradea I do not want to see this church building!' But the power and purpose of God is greater than the plans of the greatest of men. By Christmas 1989 he was dead and the work of God in Oradea and through Paul and his fellow pastor continued to flourish.

From Belfast to Romania
I trust all my writings so far about Romania, have revealed to you something of my heart. The reality is that I have come to have a special love for this the land of my adoption and sense the call of God to Romania. I have had the privilege of being called by God into ministry some fifty years ago. But once I had travelled to Romania, as I expressed earlier, that land was always in my thoughts daily. It has now become *the* mission field for me in recent years and has led to the setting up a Charity particularly focused on that country called Tell Romania.

(B) Hamilton Moore – Adjunct Professor of Emanuel

Although for the past sixteen years I have been travelling out to this country, as I explained, from 2005 I was appointed as Adjunct Professor of Emanuel Baptist University. This role has given me opportunity to live within the University and to travel throughout the country preaching, to assist in Church planting, teach on Radio Voice of the Gospel and reach out the hand of support in humanitarian aid, taking twelve 40 foot lorries so far to the country. In the introduction, I wrote of Paul finishing the course, the path mapped out for him. My own course began in Northern Ireland but the Lord has led me to Romania where now as we arrive from the UK, the friends in Emanuel can greet us with the words 'Welcome Home!'

Among the Five Percent
The spiritual needs in the country are vast. First, 87% of the people are Orthodox[64]. Only 5.4% of the people are evangelical, Baptist, Pentecostal or Christian brethren. On the other hand Jehovah Witnesses and Seventh Day Adventists are strong and the Mormons have just begun to make their presence known. We noted earlier that there are still thousands of villages without any 'gospel' witness. The work of the missionary is still vital in Romania. I am based in Emanuel, the only conservative university in all of Europe and allocated a student room. I have had the opportunity to lay biblical foundations in the minds and hearts of the students, warning them that the freedom would not just allow some to come from the West with sound theology, but there would also be a great wave of liberal thinking. They needed to be prepared to give an answer.

It was with American help the Emanuel building and Worship Chapel was erected. The opportunity was given by the Romanian Education Authority for the awarding of degrees. As we noted, Young Christians could now come to gain the necessary skills and expertise to go out into the whole country to turn things around, to minister to the social needs of so many or teach in schools and to witness to the power of the gospel as they went.

Emanuel University
Emanuel Baptist University ranks highly in my service in Romania. It is with a sense of satisfaction I look back on the years of teaching from 2005 and see young men who were once my theology students now pastoring in village and town churches in different parts of the country. In addition there are others who have been helped through their postgraduate studies at IBC under my supervision. They are either serving in different churches or are in ministry in Emanuel itself. Elijah's mantle fell upon Elisha and this is now beginning to happen in the university where others are finding a role in regular teaching. As far as I am concerned, lectures continue presently with Masters' students in New Testament Biblical Doctrine and with the 3rd and 4th year Theology students focusing on Pauline theology. In Emanuel the standards are high with each student seeking to attain excellence. These young men have a deep knowledge of the Scriptures, a passion to know God and to make the gospel known. I thank God that I can play a little part in this. The boys know they can knock the door of my student room at any time and many do.

The students also arrange many mission trips throughout the year to the south of Romania, where evangelical churches are small and few in number and the gospel is so much needed. Sundays in Emanuel can be very quiet. Many of the students are gone from 6.00 am to serve in village churches, travelling generally by bus and not returning until late. Often on Saturdays as students practise the worship songs for Sunday, or just meet at different times throughout the week to have a time of praise, the wonderful singing can be heard throughout the corridors of the university. Every Wednesday there is a special time of preaching and praise in the Chapel, when all the staff and students attend. Normally students from the different disciplines will lead the worship, whether they are from music, management, social assistance or theology. These are special times when, first we seek to talk to God in worship hymns and then, as different members of the staff or visitors to Emanuel preach, let him talk to us through his word. It is such a privilege still to be able to serve among them. They are special young people, with a spiritual vitality, who can go out into Romanian society to make a difference, whether it is in the market place, among the great social needs of the country, or in the many villages which need the gospel. Around one hundred young people will graduate every year with the vision to be used by the Lord in this land for his glory.

Just recently my ministry has extended beyond the full-time students to also include the School of Practical Theology and involvement with the Faculty of Theology staff. The School of Practical Theology emerged from the SGA School which operated in Oradea for many years in a classroom of the High School, adjacent to Emanuel Baptist Church. It was to this School that I came on that first trip on my own in 2001. Subsequently, I had opportunity to teach there on numerous occasions, especially when I was resident in the university. SGA was keen to encourage the transition of the responsibility for the teaching to evolve to local teachers. In consultation with brother Dinu Moga, who had acted as overseer and organiser of the local School for many years, a new School was organised with mainly local teachers from the university of Emanuel staff and its venue was moved there. Since I am living two floors below where the teaching is carried out it has given me the privilege of continuing to be involved along with others of the faculty. Tell Romania has been able to offer some financial support for the School and the teachers. The new School has been very helpful in providing an opportunity for those who could not study theology full-time or attend courses during the day. They are so keen to learn from God's word. During the last session I had with them on NT Theology, we looked at the theology of the cross in Paul's writings. The class lasted three hours but they were so anxious to learn that I was urged to continue for a further two hours! There is no clock watching in Romania! A one year diploma is awarded to these part-time students and their achievement is recognised as they also share in the special weekend of thanksgiving at the Annual Graduation of all students from Emanuel in late May.

My work with the Faculty of Theology staff is an important ministry. The continuing recognition of the university by the Romanian Accrediting authorities is absolutely vital. Staff therefore must progress in their own professional development. I was given the task of organising Research Forums and International Conferences which would of course help to satisfy the authorities. Written papers are being first read at the Forum, submitted to me in English for 'tweaking' and publishing in recognised journals. Conferences are being organised where both staff and students can participate.

But what about ministering in the churches? Looking back over 2015 for example, there have been so many opportunities for preaching the gospel and grounding believers in the word of God. Each Sunday is spent visiting churches, preaching in villages around Oradea and further afield. On the last few trips we had great opportunities to minister in places like Mirleau, Hidisel De Sus, Tileagd, Topa De Cris, Chistag, Cihei, Hueidin, Sanmartin, Moldova, Suceava, Medias and Decapolis.

During the years the situation has been that I have been 'based' in Emanuel. When my weekly teaching was completed, I was free to travel throughout the country, sometimes helping in the Slavic Gospel Association Schools, sometimes preaching in different churches at weekends, as I have mentioned, or taking series of meetings. It was amazing to see God at work. On one occasion I travelled with Pastor Vasile Paul of Tuga Mures to a village nearby with no real gospel witness. A believer who had a business in the village was burdened to make the gospel known. He had a hall which he had been using as a store and he invited the people to come. The rain was so heavy and the water was running past the entrance like a torrent. What do you preach to people who have never really heard the Good news before? I took them back to the beginning and told them the 'big story' from Genesis chapters one to three. Here we have the beginning of creation; the beginning of man; the beginning of sin and the beginning of the promise. Vasile challenged them to turn from their independence of God and from sin to Christ in whom they could find forgiveness and acceptance with God. I was amazed when sixteen people responded there and then!

I came to realise that I could not evangelise the whole country alone. But I could build myself into the lives of others and lay good foundations of truth and understanding – a 2 Timothy 2v1-2 strategy, the things heard from me among many witnesses impart to 'faithful men, who shall be able to teach others also'. So I would teach the Emanuel students, teach in the SGA schools, on the radio, in the local churches and preach in the villages, when I could at the weekends, looking for opportunities to encourage God's people and challenge others to repent. Another means of evangelising in Romania was to put literature into the hands of the pastors and the believers to share with others. We have read of the way God miraculously undertook for people like Brother Andrew as they brought Romanian bibles into the country. It would not have been possible to produce and hand out Gospel literature in a State which was intent on destroying religion in the country. But now the churches can grasp again the importance of sharing the Gospel in written form. Such literature goes back to apostolic days – see the main purpose of John's Gospel in John 20v30-31 or realise that Mark's Gospel is simply 'the gospel of Jesus Christ, the Son of God', (Mk. 1v1) in written form. So I was able to select a number of tracts and booklets. These were warnings of the false teachings of Jehovah Witnesses or particularly for young people a booklet on the pornography trap. I also wrote a leaflet on John 3v16 and got it translated. Every Home Crusade printed them for me – first eight million, which we shared with a Brethren Evangelist, Paul Williams, then again, four hundred thousand. Recently it was a joy to make them available for students to take home to their churches or picked up in Emanuel by young pastors. I was able to distribute them at the Communitatea (the monthly meeting of eighty pastors in the Bihor County of Romania) and send them to different regions of Romania, Suceava, Medias, Cluj.

'Two are better than one…'

When Elieen went home to heaven I found that continuing to focus upon my work in IBC helped me greatly. My youngest daughter was still at home (with her dog Spot!), which meant I was never alone. Then when I was released from my full time commitment to the College in 2010, I devoted my life completely to the work in Romania. The work began to develop, and with the help of Pastor David McFarland we set up the web site, tellromania.org. We formed a charity with three other Directors, Jeff and Carol Stevenson, my daughter Pamela and myself. I was often alone in Emanuel, especially at the weekends, when I was not somewhere in a village preaching. I kept in touch with my family, Wendy, David and Pamela (and my grandchildren) using Skype. Yet I can testify that I was never alone for I had a real sense of God's presence with me. Although the work of Tell Romania was small at the beginning and mainly focused on my own preaching and teaching, it was set to expand. For a couple of years we were able to send out just one lorry with humanitarian aid. But in the past eighteen months we actually sent twelve 40 – 45ft lorries with supplies to needy situations such as the following: hospitals received a quarter of a million pounds worth of equipment all donated to us; the Felix Orphan community in Oradea mentioned earlier; furnishings, bedding, sanitary ware and a fully equipped commercial kitchen for the Racatau Mountain Retreat Centre planned by Betel Baptist Church, Cluj; household items and clothing for Roma communities in Odoreu and Cluj and five dental treatment centres and instruments.

Two other men from Northern Ireland came alongside to help, David Morton and Freddie Smyth. They had been in Iris Baptist Church in Cluj helping with some projects where I was preaching one Sunday evening. When the service was over, I heard a voice a few rows back with a Northern Ireland accent. That's how we met and they offered to assist me when back in Northern Ireland. I still remember David saying to me on one occasion, 'You do the preaching and we will do the fetching'. So with their help we were able to move our place for storing items from brother Mark Wilson's farm outside Banbridge to set up a new store near to them in Ballyclare. They came on board as new Directors. But a very special Director joined them – one who would be constantly at my side in the future. Yes, two are certainly better than one.

That change occurred in my life on the occasion of my marriage to Shirley on 22nd October 2012. Having returned home at the end of June, I did not return to Romania alone. Shirley was my pianist in Castlereagh for many years, where she and her husband Douglas were members. We both had known the pain of bereavement. Shirley never had the opportunity to visit Romania before our wedding. I jokingly said I was not sure what would happen when in travelling out with me, she stepped off the plane and declared this was not her calling. But that was not the outcome; God makes no mistakes. He had placed Romania heavily upon her heart. She explained to me that she did not wish to go to Romania simply as my wife, to care and look after me, but wanted the Lord to give her a work of her own, something she could personally do for him. Right from the first trip together it was obvious that Shirley was loved by the female students in Emanuel University. Her ministry quickly developed as in the Beauty of Holiness Group, in the work of the Emanuel Hospice Home Care ministry and in the Child-life Romania ministry. Shirley has a compelling passion for her children, her girls! Dr. Peter Firth accompanying me on a recent visit remarked on the love and affection evident for Sister Shirley (as she is known in Romania) both by faculty and students. This is clear for all to see, but then again, she is 'At Home'. So I have had the special God-given privilege of loving and being loved by two wonderful women in my life.

God has also given Shirley and myself opportunities in radio ministry. The local station, Radio Voice of the Gospel, Oradea continues to welcome us to teach various subjects on a regular basis. Whether it is a series on Easter, or God's wonderful salvation, redemption, justification, reconciliation or adoption, or studies in worship, we are always welcome – or with Shirley introducing Irish and English recipes, but using the opportunity to share the gospel as well. We have an open door. But there is another special ministry.

Compelled by love alone
We have recounted the revival that began in Emanuel Baptist Church in Oradea when Liviu Olah first came. As I explained, the church has continued to know blessing and has now 4,000 members, plus a number of significant Christian ministries; the Christian High School, Bethesda Medical Centre for the poor; Casa Grace, a ministry for orphan children, Emanuel University, separate from the State, totally independent, under the authority of the Church and also, another very important ministry, Emanuel Hospice. The Hospice has a team of twelve – one doctor and five nurses, four administration staff, including the director, one psychologist, also a social worker. At this moment they have no hospice building although the Town Hall has now

allocated to them a piece of land and work is in progress to provide accommodation for seventeen adults and seven children. Therefore all treatment has to be carried out in the homes of the patients. Their Annual Report for 2014 states that during that year the Hospice provided palliative care at home for 327 patients (285 adults and 42 children). The medical team together with the psycho-social team made 6,781 visits to patients. It is very emotional work to minister in love to the terminally ill, children and adults, especially when one loses a child. In my earlier years in Emanuel I could only visit the Hospice team when taking some money as the Lord led. But during these past three years since Shirley has come into my life, she has become directly involved at every level with a number of patients, (adult and children) visiting and encouraging them. I smiled on hearing one of the patients say, 'Sister Shirley, you keep coming back'. Her reply was, 'I will always be back, you are loved'. Shirley is driven by a passion, a level of care for 'other little ships' that are treasured and valued by her, recognising the responsibility and to whom she is answerable. She has been able to raise financial support from individuals in Northern Ireland for the monthly feeding programme, scans, medicines, chemotherapy, even some funds to partially pay for a bone marrow transplant. During one of our 'early morning conversations' she shared how she has traced the rainbow through the cloud when longing for a family of her own; now years later the Lord has given her hundreds to love and cherish. She is compelled by love alone.

This is so evident in her ministry with Child-Life Romania, a ministry twinned with the Hospice, where child-life specialists have the opportunity to care for the children in the local hospital by the art of play on three afternoons a week. There are two specialists at the moment, but the aim is to expand this ministry to other hospitals. In November 2015, Tell Romania was able to send a 45 ft lorry of medical equipment, plus many boxes of new or nearly new clothes for children and babies, plus buggies, car seats and cots to be used in this work. This ministry is very dear to Shirley's heart.

To help illustrate the "heart" of her ministry, I include some of Shirley's blogs[65] from the recent past. These reveal some of the challenges to faith and the amazing opportunities that have been given to both of us.

Shirley's Blogs

Little Lambs posted on March 20th 2015 by Shirley

'Spring, she has come, yes?' I was amazed to find the tight green buds had burst overnight into an array of golden daffodils. 'Beautiful', I replied. I was glad of this distraction, reminding myself that everything in nature is beautiful for a season preceded by a time of preparation yielding provision and attaining perfection.

'What times I am afraid, I will trust in You'. I am not gifted, achievements? Just driven to walk His footsteps in this pathway of service and one that I personally find difficult. Many visits, opportunities this week I need to embrace the responsibility of sharing that the end is not the end but only the beginning.

Jonut, Calin, Cristian, Andrei, Ana Maria and little Marian – the children of Mia, who is now at home with the Lord. Daria and I had a special time with the children as they shared their 'Family Album' – the little one smiling as he said 'Mummy'. One cannot help but see, sense, the sadness, the emptiness, yet they smile so bravely, asking you: 'When you come back in April, please come again, you are welcome'. Brother Florin – an amazing story of grace – as he now waits to face his fourth surgery related to his terminal illness. My time with this family was precious. I am always asked 'Where is your husband?' They listen with interest as I share the everydayness of life back home, assuring them of our love and passion for this, their land, the land of Romania. Sister Magdelina, living alone and unable to leave her flat is to be my next port of call.

Estera and I also made 'visits' and off we went! I noticed the beautiful white fleecy lamb on her windscreen. 'Shirley, you remember little Beni?' I could never forget him – I can still hear him repeat his memory verse at the Hospice Christmas Celebration – he was called home on 28th December 2014. Yet, even at 9 years of age, he asked if he could be baptised before he met Jesus! He gave his little lamb to Estera. 'Please remember me'! We had arrived at Oradea Hospital and made our way to the Haematology Ward where I met Denisa a 22 year-old Medical student suffering from Leukaemia. We chatted and I learned of her plans and ambitions for the future, as she talked, I noticed the sadness portrayed through the eyes of her loving Mother – her Ewe Lamb was very sick. Galatians 5: 22-23 came to mind: 'But the fruit of the Spirit is love, joy, peace, patience, kindness, goodness, faithfulness, gentleness ……' Please take a moment to whisper her name in prayer.

Not only did my head ache but my heart ached – emotionally drained after days of pain and sadness, where devastating news changes and shatters lives forever. I ask you to remember Sister Marinela Murg, Director. Emanuel Hospice, provides free of charge palliative care services at home for the dying in their community. Through their dedication, devotion and calling they were able to make a difference in the lives of 285 adult patients and 42 children during 2014. Please pray the Lord will enable this work to again reach and touch many lives during 2015 to share God's love and compassion to the patients God will entrust into their care. – The cost of discipleship! Questions, so many questions. Am I connected enough to make a difference? Am I prepared to 'Go the Distance?'

As I meet with the various staff in the Hospice, they have shared how they personally have been encouraged to keep on casting their bread upon the waters through my husband's weekly messages at their prayer time.

Yesterday, the children of the Art Therapy Class in the Municipal Hospital painted a beautiful Irish Shamrock with a message reading: 'Happy Saint Patrick's Day Mrs Shirley' with all their little names recorded on the back! Will thank them personally next Tuesday. We can touch lives in all manner of ways – I am getting there, they know I love them – and I do! Yes, (for me) it is hard to serve in this area of sensitivity – yet 'His' presence is so real as I listen, share or play – all different – yet all filled with the emptiness circumstances of change have brought and for many brought prematurely.

Joshua, Dragos, David, Julia, again some of the names so precious to my heart in another Art Therapy Class held today, Thursday, for the bereaved children. We made four different Caterpillars – one Happy, one Sad, one Fearful, one Angry – through this form of therapy the children can vent their inner feelings. This was followed by Medical or Hospital Therapy when each child received a Rag Doll – Daria asked each one to paint a face on their individual doll. I found this most informative as I quietly watched from afar their reaction.

On arriving home at room 205 – an email was waiting to confirm that Mr. Paul Russell (RVH/Jubilee Maternity Hospital) had donated six Basinettes and Consumables to the new project Child Life Romania. 'Before You Call' … We have shared with Sister Raelene this morning and she is amazed and encouraged through this provision. As I write, an army of Students (led by 'The Professor') are placing the many boxes sent previously by Paul – yet we were unaware of our involvement in this particular area. And so we rest in His plan and purpose knowing that all the projects were answered last year and trust for the days ahead as new doors of opportunity open before us.

Container Number five finally reached its destination, the contents of which were to facilitate eight outlets – Dr. Moore was so grateful to Pastor Filip Faragu for his time and patience in leading the team at Cluj.

Dr. Moore continues to lecture, preach, record Easter Messages on Radio Voice of the Gospel and send various sermons to Pastor David McFarland to place on 'Tell Out The Truth' http://tellromania.org This week-end we head to Satu Mare and Odoreu for a Mission Trip (leaving 5.00 am your time). The book on the Pastoral Epistles is submitted, we need to prayerfully consider translation into Romanian and Hungarian languages. Book number two already in process – Galatians.

Four weeks? Eleven Days remaining in this Mission Trip. Pray we will be effective, obedient Servants 'Unto Him'. These have been days of discovery, waiting before the Lord, seeing His plan unfold in many miraculous ways – ways we never imagined! We will be home for a few days at Easter then back again to our second home? Perhaps first home? Shirley

We were not home for long. The next blog reveals the opportunities in Scueava first of all, then Pecieu and Odoreu in April 2015. Shirley reflects on what God is continuing to do through us.

Portstewart-Belfast-Dublin-Bacau-Suceava – 21 Hours Posted by Shirley 24th April 2015

In the words of Elisabeth Elliot *'This job has been given me to do, therefore, it is a gift, therefore, it is a privilege, therefore it is an offering I may make to God, therefore, it is to be done gladly, if it is done for Him. Here, not somewhere else, I may learn God's Way, in this job, not in some other, God looks for faithfulness'.*

Suceava has proved to be days filled with momentous events, tremendous challenges and endless opportunities. Our choice, our desire remains unchanged – to give ourselves to a Christ Directed Service. Psalm 62v5. 'My soul wait silently for God alone….'. We wait quietly trusting day by day.

It was great to spend these ten days with Pastor Catalin Croitor and his wife Paula – Catalin had a planned schedule and our days were filled ministering, commencing Saturday morning visiting various youth ministries etc. Sunday brought the opportunity to preach in two village churches, one a remote Roma village. Monday through Friday, amazing days of sharing with Pastors, Young Married Group, 500 High School Students, Men's Bible Class – combining some home visits: Catella (77) living alone in a block of flats where she is the only tenant – her days are long and lonely 'do you know an elderly person who needs looking after?' she asked – her loving heart always thinking of others. A village, similar to Odoreu where we spent time with a sickly, single Mum with eleven children – existing – one room with only a bucket to fetch water and a stove to cook (when they can afford to eat)!

The week passed quickly and it was time for the Slavic Gospel Association to commence Friday evening – all day Saturday, some travelled sixty kms to attend. Tomorrow we minister in Betleehem Church, then another long drive of ten hours to Pecieu for Dr. Moore and Oradea for me. Dr. Moore will lecture in the second SGA School Monday through to Wednesday when hopefully we will meet on Thursday morning when we will then drive to Satu Mare for a three day Mission in Odoreu – then back to Emanuel University for a few days before Irlande De Nord for a short five day trip home before returning again (via Spain, then on to Emanuel) until mid June.

My own days of opportunity highlighted the increasing awareness that I do have a job to do and that I must do it well. Anything I do, wouldn't be, shouldn't be, couldn't be enough (thank you Bernie).

Iochebed Centre (advising against Abortion) where I met Gabi and Mihala, two sisters whose love goes beyond as they counsel, personally touch and answer every knock on their door from young girls as young as thirteen. Distress, Fear is replaced with Hope and a Future. Their ministry of care, support extends to eight villages where cots, food, firewood, whatever is needed even to bricks they bring it! Their job is special! I saw the reality as three girls entered just as I was leaving. The girls showed me a picture taken during December in the snow – yes, the little ones were cute! But they had no socks or shoes?????????????

'Lord, why? How? Can you eliminate my questions? Thoughts still revolving inside, I arrived back at the flat to find my husband had already left for another meeting as I sat alone reflecting, talking to the Lord and asking Him ' Lord, Show Me, Tell Me'. I opened my Bible at 1 Peter 4: 10, 11: ' *As each one has received a gift minister it one to another… if anyone ministers let him do it as with the ability which God supplies*'. Pastor David McFarland had shared this passage with me (by mobile telephone) as we were travelling to Belfast. I called to mind the telephone call as I was boarding the coach for Dublin! Three hours later, my husband returned. 'Shirley, would you like me to try to access your emails?' Aware of the difficulties I doubted the success! Five emails were waiting – Hazel, Gillian, Jackie, Tracey, Margaret all regarding CHILD LIFE ROMANIA! Many Individuals, BWF, Groups are collecting – I am so overwhelmed, so encouraged as I stand back in awe of this provision. 'Thank You' for staying close beside TELL ROMANIA – it is as it says: TELL R O M A N I A and so wherever, whatever God sends we will be 'Good Stewards' – we only want what God wants us to have and for His glory! Our next container will leave during September – can you, will you help this project to offer hope, refuge to Child Life Romania, Iochebed, Hospice Children, Gypsy Children – there is food for all!

JOB 31: 16 -22. '*If I have caused the eyes of the widow to fail …If I have seen anyone perish for lack of clothing …If I have raised my hand against the fatherless, when I saw I had help in the gate; then let my arm fall from my shoulder, let my arm be torn from the socket*'.

God continues to fill our hand with work. The Update of March 2016 includes something of my ongoing responsibilities and the bonds of fellowship Shirley is making with the female students of Emanuel.

Posted on March 1st 2016 by Shirley
It is a glorious morning; the air is crisp. I smile as I walk briskly down the long and winding path to Emanuel Chapel where the sunlight is streaming

through the beautiful window depicting 'The Sower'. Why am I smiling? I notice tiny buds peering through the hard and frosty ground uniting in a majestic declaration 'Winter Is Passing'. My mind turns immediately to Song of Songs 2: 10-13 '…Lo, the winter is past, the rain is over and gone, the flowers appear on the earth, the time of the singing of the birds is come … Arise, my love, my fair one, and come away'. Come Away? Yes 'The Moores' have 'Come Away' – away to a land of great need, heartache, poverty, sickness and pain – pain that no medication can remove.

David Livingstone in his dairy penned: 'The strangest disease I have found in this country seems really to be broken-heartedness'. No one is exempt, young, old, rich or poor. Dr. Moore and I have one obligation to serve with love that is without limit!

The blessing of this trip commenced from day one with many 'fruitful days'. We plan, prepare, prioritise the really important from the important, but if we could see beyond today; if for one moment we could see with our natural eye the end result – surely our minds would be 'hushed' into quiet submission to the Master Plan. Within one journey of my favourite eight flights of stairs, EVERYONE I needed to contact was either 'going up' or 'going down'. Incredible? But then we know who is in charge, we know the One who rules with stupendous power, who is unique, triumphant and ALIVE today!

These have been 'fruitful days' – I am compelled to serve knowing that today is the yesterday I will remember tomorrow and so with the Psalmist I cry: 'Teach Us To Number Our Days'. Each day should be a fruitful day – as we, the seasons of spring, summer, autumn pass, grow old – may we never lose our 'freshness' for the gospel.

I have so much to be thankful for: 'My Girls' (as I affectionately call them) from the Beauty of Holiness Group are a blessing in their zeal and hunger after God. Please remember Oana, Ligia, Ana, Ema, Alina, Dina, Anca & Tabita –they are precious to me and I shall miss them as I say 'Good Bye' this evening. Yes, I am sad. You see I have come to love them as they have been given to me to care for and nurture in the things of the Lord. Our small student room did not cease yesterday and today with the 'young ones' calling with a White Tulip, Plants as today is 'ladies day' in Romania! Precious Memories in my heart. Thank You Girls!

Silvia who heads the Child Life Romania Team was excited and encouraged as we met, sharing that the team have access into the hospital wards three afternoons each week – pray for Silvia and her team of volunteers as they show their love for people who need the Lord, that these children, teenagers and parents will know, will feel the warmth of everlasting arms surrounding them.

The Students of Emanuel University are close to my heart – as I scan the flock, the potential! Lord, drive me onward to serve day by day, to give, to leave something for Thee!

Marinela, Estera and I met this week. We reflected on our first meeting together and of my introduction to Romania. Clearly the Lord led me to the Hospice and since the fall of this year I have been searching my heart; yes, I am only one but I want so much to help this amazing team. A team who are a Balm! Devoted and dedicated in their love and care.

Pastor David McFarland has produced a magnificent presentation with a new window on the Feeding Programme (photographs of a few families), a current update on Denisa (recent photograph) and a new window of meditation – well worth a visit! His passion and devotion to Tell Romania is evident in his attention to detail. I will be sharing reports once little Ella and Elizabeth have various tests and scans duly completed.

Dr. Moore also writes in the blog:
I am 'Back Home' in the place where I belong! God continues to open many doors of opportunity.

It was great to be back with the young Theology Students as they seek to deepen their understanding of God's Word. The past two weeks have been spent in teaching third and fourth year. It is encouraging to see their growth and the awareness of a deep bond of friendship.

The Research Forum was held on 23rd Feb. as arranged – it is important to meet together as lecturers to share our theological interests and progress. I am tasked to read the articles which are being written for publication in English, as they must be.

We feel the need to share one with the other and so I am in the process of arranging an International Conference on Friday, 6th May 2016 in

Emanuel University Chapel. This will take the form of a Theological Conference focusing on 'The Epistle to the Hebrews in the New Testament: Its Historical Context and Theological Significance'. Speakers include Dr. Paul Negrut, Rector of Emanuel University, Dr. Peter Firth, Irish Baptist College, along with myself and other guests who will be invited to deliver a paper. The afternoon will give the students also the opportunity to present short papers as well. I will choose a number of the articles for publication in a special Journal.

Pastor Daniel Tanc made contact regarding the Radio Voice of the Gospel and we set time aside yesterday for a recording on the theme of Worship.

This morning I was invited to speak at the meeting of the Communitate where approximately fifty Pastors meet each month for prayer and worship. Andrei, one of my third year Theology Students assisted in preparing boxes of books printed by Evangelical Press from the pallet we brought out on the last lorry, plus the Romanian tracts and booklets – 400,000 donated by Every Home Crusade. It was such a joy to see the eager response of the pastors as they 'carried' the boxes/tracts to their car to take back to their churches and villages. The morning was a blessed time together with many new and old faces! Great to catch up with Pastor Remus, Satu Mare and to meet former Theological Students and new brethren who are anxious for me to visit their church on my return.

And so, it is time to go! I like Shirley will be sad to leave 'My Boys'! There is much to accomplish in my time at home as I continue the writing of my future books and we put plans in action for the forthcoming May.

Confirmation has just been received that Shirley will have surgery at 12 noon on Friday (2pm Romanian Time) – just remember her as I know where her heart lies and longs to be.

Thank You for your love and support. 'The Moores' 01st March 2016 One important aspect of the Hospice ministry is feeding the children in some cases to the end of their lives. Shirley's blog reflects a call for support for the feeding programme to which there was an amazing response.

The Hungry Fed, the Humble Lifted High!
Posted on February 1st 2016 by Shirley
The words of this hymn sung last night in church pierced my heart! Only hours earlier I had received an email from my friend Marinela Murg (Director of Emanuel Hospice Homecare Team), Oradea, Romania. As I read the contents, my emotion(s) became one of concern after the initial shock!

Many adults/children receive loving care, medication, and in some cases, dignity until their final days! Thirty patients and families are carefully evaluated and selected – those who are terminally ill and struggle financially.

One Food Parcel each month is not only a necessity but a blessing – a Gift from Above!
Marinela confirmed as from 31st January, specifically designated funds have reached completion! There is no money to buy food parcels for these precious families (our brothers and sisters). As individuals we cannot feed all thirty but we can perhaps feed one! £15 per month will feed one family = £500 (in total) will feed all thirty!

Three years ago, I married Dr. Moore. His words still vivid in my memory when he asked in his own quiet manner 'Shirley, will you come with me to Romania?' – For one who had only flown once in her lifetime, my answer was without hesitation! 'I will go, but only if the Lord gives me a work of my own'. Impossible circumstances for one who struggles with emotion – God makes no mistakes!

The Hospice work is my passion – but then I have found the more passion you have for God the more compassion He gives you for others! I leave for Romania on Wednesday, 17th February for a shorter visit than planned as I have been informed this morning I need to return home for hand surgery. Today is the 2nd February – will you help 'Feed the Hungry' this month?

The mark of reality of a true disciple: Matthew 25: 35 'For I was hungry and you gave Me food, I was thirsty and you gave Me drink; I was a stranger and you took Me in'.

Shirley

The next blog recorded the great response made to this need in the Feeding Programme. It is clear that God was at work to meet the needs of the oppressed.

Windbreak, Watershed? Posted on February 27, 2016 by Shirley

The words of Deuteronomy 32: 2 regulate the pendulum of life swinging from fear and anxiety to faith and trust.*'He is the Rock; His work is perfect. Everything He does is perfect. Everything He does is just and fair. He is a faithful God ......'*

What a promise to commence my morning! I am surrounded, watched over and guarded – but then isn't that how we care for our most precious possession?

Waiting isn't easy! Tick Tock! Tick Tock! Clock Watching! I am waiting for Marinela and Estera – longing to hear their 'gentle knock' on the door of room 205, their amazing smile as we meet again – we are 'friends' we are 'sisters' and love to share together!

I pause, thinking of the words found further down in our chapter: 'He nourished, He fed, He gave, and gave only from the choicest of wheat!' During these past two weeks, I have been on a journey of discovery, discovering the unfathomable faithfulness of God, proving that His words are never idle words, but are in fact – Life with a capital 'L' in all its fullness! 'The Hungry Fed, The Humble Lifted High'. The Hospice Feeding Programme!!!!!!!!!!!!!

Through those whose hearts the Lord touched, TELL ROMANIA forwarded to Marinela Murg (Director) this morning, sufficient funding to provide for six months. The thirty families carefully evaluated by Estera (Social Worker) will now receive a monthly food parcel knowing that the shared ministry of brothers and sisters in Northern Ireland, who responded, is indeed a shared blessing – thank you! You have become a shelter, a place of quiet rest, a river of refreshing waters, a shadow in the cleft of the rock where safety and security can be found from the stormy winds that blow our way in this earthly life.

On a personal note, thank you for caring, loving, understanding, through your humility to serve, to share their grief, sorrow and loss, their poverty & pain, you have become His Hands, His Feet, You have become 'Christ to Them'.

My husband and I remain humble, clearly recognising that Christ became a man and laid aside the Glory He had known, to become a lowly Carpenter! But God exalted Him – The Humble Lifted High! We all pass through deep waters at some time in life but remember – it is 'when' not 'if' – 'through' not 'into' I will be with you! (Isa. 43:2) Shirley, 26/02/2016.

Excursus: The Hospice Leaflet

The ministry of the staff at Emanuel Hospice is such an important means of support for the most needy in the whole Bihor County. Just recently I felt exercised to write a leaflet for the terminally ill, which, with the help of one of my students, was printed by Every Home Crusade. The tract entitled, 'News You Do Not Want To Hear', is now available for the Hospice staff to take on their visits and also is being used by the students in Emanuel when involved in weekly practical work for those under Hospice care. Someone who is reading this book may be in a similar situation and in need of the help and assurance which is here outlined:

News we do not want to Hear.
We read in the book of Psalms 'Have no fear of bad news'. Yet to be personally diagnosed with a terminal illness is shattering and life changing. Suddenly our focus, our purpose in life has changed affecting the lives of our loved ones. We are overwhelmed, our hearts filled with fear as we face the future ahead, perhaps without a Father, Mother, Son, Daughter, or Grandparent. The Arms of Mercy reach out to you offering you love, care from devoted and dedicated people who can offer Medical, Social and Psychological care. You need to know there are those who will care for you throughout your illness, sharing their spiritual relationship with God, as you walk through this dark and difficult experience. This life is but a moment in time and is a gift from the Hand of God. Your name is engraved on the palm of His hand and He knows you by name.

In John 9v1-3 Jesus makes clear the teaching that every sickness is the result of individual sin of the sick person is wrong and unbiblical. He says, 'Neither has this man sinned nor his parents' that he was born blind. Sickness and death are the result of the fall of man in the Garden of Eden and they can come into any life and family. Through Adam's one sin 'death passed upon all men', Romans 5v12.

Where can we find hope? Our hearts need to be open for help from every source including medical help. And there is always help available in God. He has purposed that one day death, pain and sickness will be no more, 'for God shall wipe away all tears from their eyes', Revelation 21v4. We ask: 'What can I do, where do I go when I am overwhelmed by fear?'

Cry out to Him and put yourself in His hands. He is the one who can bring healing – present or ultimate, in His time and in His purpose and plan.

Accept that God has the power to heal, but this does not always happen. Paul prayed but still remained sick; 2 Corinthians 12v7-10; Trophimus was sick and was not healed, 2 Timothy 4v20. It depends on His sovereign plan for us.

Remember that God promised to bring us finally into ultimate healing. Martha had wanted immediate healing for her brother when he fell ill, but Jesus said 'I am the resurrection and the life. He who believes in me even though he dies he will live. And whoever lives and believes in me will never die', John 11v25-26.

Realise that as sinners we can never make ourselves right with God. No works, or what we could give of our money can make things right. But when we could do nothing, God did everything – He gave His own son to die in the place of sinners and He paid the price in full on the cross.

Believe that all that needs to be done, Jesus on the cross did it for us; depend upon Him and not on yourself.

Turn from your sinful way and submit to Him who is the living Christ. He will accept you and give to you the certainty that one day you will be with Him, delivered from all pain and sickness. John 6v37 'the one who comes to me I will never cast out'. We have been like sheep going astray but you can now return to Him who is 'the Shepherd and Overseer of our souls', 1 Peter 2v24-25. He will watch over you and be a Shepherd to be with you always, to care for and support you as you depend upon Him.

Rest in Him, depend on His promises as you find them revealed in His word, since your life now belongs to God. He has promised, 'I will never leave you nor forsake you. So we may boldly say, "The Lord is my helper; I will not fear. What can man do to me?"' Hebrews 13v5-6.

There is one and there are many, and you are one who is loved and precious. We want you to know we will remember you, praying that His strength will be made perfect in your weakness.

Hamilton & Shirley Moore

(C) Hamilton Moore – Founder of Tell Romania

tellromania.org

When the Lord revealed his will through 'Gideon's Fleece', I could not ignore it. My whole focus since then has become centred on ministry in Romania. Nothing has happened over the past six years to question this commitment. It has been said, 'Do not enter the ministry unless you cannot help it'. The idea is that you will never be happy doing anything else. This is true for my life and that of my wife Shirley. We are content – and would never be content if we were not in the hollow of his hand, in the place of his choosing and are sure that God has brought us together 'for such a time as this'. One verse which has meant a lot to us is Jeremiah 29v11 ESV, 'For I know the plans I have for you, declares the Lord, plans for welfare and not for evil, to give you a future and a hope'. Being available to him is all that matters.

As I reflect on this I am reminded of the same emphasis on direction in ministry in the mission of God which is found in John 20-21. John 21 forms an epilogue at the end of the Gospel which balances the prologue of 1v1-18. Here the third appearance of Christ, risen from the dead is recorded; the words in v14 'the 3rd time' shows this, an appearance in Galilee, by the sea of Tiberius. The first emphasis here is that he is risen! But risen with what to do? In the story as we look at Peter we will see that Jesus was risen to direct his church, his people in the ongoing mission of God.

Peter and the Seven were GIVING UP. It was a critical time for the twelve and for Peter. He decides he is going to fish. This incident has given rise to a lot of discussion. Most are not prepared to be critical of the seven. But I believe there is reason to consider that here the disciples were in a period of uncertainty about the plan, the way, the will of God. Here we see:

The Risen Lord GOING AFTER them. Here Jesus went after them because he wanted them for his church. They were important people in his plan. He had greater plans for them all than just catching a few fish. Jesus had said to them earlier in Luke 5v1-11, in a similar situation, 'From henceforth thou shalt catch men', v10. The Lord had greater work for Peter than to be in the old boat, see Acts 2v41 where he would see three thousand and in 4v4 five thousand 'in the net'.

The Lord was on the shore; he had come and in fact was GUIDING THEM. He was there to teach them lessons for the future, lessons about fishing for men. In v5 it is recorded 'that night they caught nothing'. Why was this? Were they not good fishermen? Had they lost the skill? The answer is on the shore. He is not only the Lord of angels and demons but of all creation, even little fish. It was no accident that they caught nothing. They had to learn an important lesson. The best skill, exercised in the most promising circumstances is no guarantee of success outside his will. So Jesus says, 'Cast the net on the right side ... and thou shalt find', v 6. There were scores of fish so that the net was about to break. The lesson for the future was – since he was sending them in the mission of God as God the Father had sent him (John 20v21) – that all service must be Christ-directed. It really was a parable for the future when Jesus would command 'go and teach all nations'; 'beginning at Jerusalem...'.

Therefore as we have sought to plan, we must be open to the Lord to guide. Our conviction is that we are not in Tell Romania to work for God, but seeking to keep low in allowing him to work through us. To him be all the glory for anything that has been accomplished! He has accomplished it. We need constantly to be open to him as to where we will work and live. The disciples learned the important truth that apart from Christ they can do nothing, 15v5. And so must we. He is no longer on the shore, but in heaven and can still direct.

So the Lord led me to set up the work of Tell Romania in March 2012. The charity had a number of aims and objectives:

- To assist in the teaching and training of individuals for Christian service in Eastern Europe, particularly Romania.
- To engage in evangelism, support translation and the production of Christian literature.
- To assist local churches in their Christian ministry.
- To provide humanitarian aid.

We are just two people at the moment but with a team of helpers. The website http://tellromania.org created and maintained by Pastor David McFarland keeps people informed of needs and of upcoming events. A Tell the Truth section provides sermon notes and teaching material to all who log on. Having preached for fifty years and taught in the Irish Baptist College for twenty I wish to leave a legacy which others can use and from which many can benefit. Much so far has been accomplished but it is only the beginning.

In keeping with the aims of Tell Romania to 'support translation and the production of Christian literature', my book, *1 & 2 Timothy and Titus: Missional Texts from a Great Missionary Statesman* is now in process of being translated and the aim is to have it published for the pastors, students and elders of particularly Baptist and Pentecostal Churches. My vision is that this will be the first of many, as God enables.

PART THREE: Why This Story?

WE HAVE COME to the end of my story – for the present. I pray God that he may yet – if the day of grace is extended even more – allow me to continue to serve him. But I must emphasise my purpose in producing this whole autobiography. I want God to get the glory and you to be blessed and encouraged in seeing how God has worked in an ordinary life in what I would consider are extraordinary ways. As you have been informed about the great need in Romania and have learnt what God is doing – the power overcoming the pain, I pray that you are challenged to respond personally to God in allowing him to be God in your life so that you also can be his instrument in the mission of God, when and where he wills.

I finish this book by reminding you of what Paul and Jesus have said.

What Paul Wrote 2 Tim.4v1-13

This section was written to Timothy by the great Apostle Paul. He was in prison and awaiting the final judgment of the Roman Court. It was clear in all of 2 Timothy that Paul was about to hand on the torch, to urge Timothy to take the apostolic gospel to the next generation. This was also true as far as Titus was concerned, (Tit. 1v4-5; 2v1, 7; 3v1-2, 12-14). This is my own burden for the land of Romania and is one of the motives for the writing of this book – to set others on fire to share the gospel wherever God has planned for them to go. 1 & 2 Timothy and Titus emphasise Paul's warnings not to divert from the true gospel but to preach it clearly.[66] The local church in Ephesus and those in Crete were to make known that message. They had a responsibility in the mission of God where God had placed them and they must not only preach the message but live it out; their lifestyle must reflect the power of the message through their own transformation. Here is a summary of what Paul wrote concerning our responsibility. They are in fact the last recorded words of Paul.

The Final Charge v.1-5 'I charge thee therefore before God...' Paul is standing in full view of the court of heaven – before God and Christ Jesus – as he commits the charge to Timothy. He must take the gospel to the next generation. The charge was also in light of the second coming of Christ, who will judge the living and the dead. Timothy's work will be recalled and he must give account. His life – in fact the ministry of us all in the mission of God – is on display before God and Christ. The charge focuses upon preaching, v.2. Romania has had, and must continue to have powerful preaching. But what to preach? 'Preach the word'. Timothy will know what Paul is referring to – the apostolic body of doctrine passed on from Paul; the God-breathed Scriptures (2 Tim. 3v16) Timothy had been taught them since he had been a child. Matthew Henry[67] notes: 'Not our own notions or fancies we are to preach, but the pure plain Word of God'. He was to 'preach' it; to proclaim or herald the word, not just deliver a moral or religious discourse of any kind and in any way i.e., in the weakened sense in which 'preach' is often understood today. Timothy was actually being encouraged to take Paul's place in the ongoing mission of God. Is there someone whose place you can take in mission ministry in Romania or elsewhere?

This is an urgent proclamation. So Timothy must be urgent 'in season, out of season'. Men and women are on their way to God's eternity! How can we not be in earnest about souls? Timothy must convey the urgent importance of what he is preaching. Also, he is to be on duty at all times. When the time is convenient and when it is not convenient. Paul seemed to be in an 'out of season' situation in prison, but he still preached the word. Timothy is not to be timid but is to 'reprove, rebuke and exhort' with the full authority and sufficiency of the Scriptures. He is to do so 'with all longsuffering and doctrine'. Christian reproof without the grace of longsuffering has often led to a harsh, censorious attitude intensely harmful to the cause of Christ. Second, his teaching should involve the most painstaking and thorough style of instruction. Timothy's preaching was not just to be mainly made up of little stories, almost all illustrative material (important as it is) but solid doctrine.

It is clear that before the coming of Christ there were going to be dark days. People would not be able to bear the truth. 'They will not endure sound doctrine' but accumulate teachers according to their own desires. They pile them up, teacher upon teacher. People more and more in Romania, as in other places of the world will prefer the sensational and the speculative, rather than good doctrine which would build them up. The word 'itching' ears, is used figuratively of curiosity that looks for interesting and spicy bits of information or what is sensational or novel. The false teachers will scratch the itching ears. Timothy needed to be teaching the truth (sound teaching) because wholesome doctrine was becoming more and more unpopular, but it was what the people of God needed to build them up. Once the Ephesians left the straight road of truth, the fanciful fables and myths might satisfy their disorientated imaginations (see 1 Tim. 1v3-4). But they do not seem aware that truth has been left behind. So as for Timothy, he is to be different. He must not take his lead from the prevailing 'theological fashions' of the day. This is vital teaching and advice for Timothy and for us all. People in the local church need to be grounded in the truth and built up.

In v5 Timothy must watch in all things, be clear-minded, have a true appreciation of the situation and watch out for the danger of falling into sin. He must 'endure afflictions', be prepared to be unpopular and to 'do the work of an evangelist'. The good news is to be spread abroad. Today we must not lose the vision of local and world-wide need, including Romania! Making 'full proof' means that Timothy is to fully fulfil his ministry here set out by Paul. The mission of God must continue.

The Final Chapter v.6-8 Most commentators call this section Paul's 'last will and testament'. Paul's ministry is reaching its conclusion. Timothy is to step into the gap. The apostle's example, now set out is to be his younger colleague's template.

Paul likens his life to a libation or drink offering being poured out. Paul's whole life had been a sacrifice. Now he faced the supreme sacrifice and uses another word to point to his death, the word 'departure'. We should note that death for the Christian is simply a departure to heaven and Paul saw his death as his finest hour. Paul's motive here in writing as he does is simply to provide encouragement for Timothy.

He looks back over thirty years of ministry and describes it factually, not boastfully, with three metaphorical statements of its usefulness. *The Fight* – 'a good fight' – Paul had earlier encouraged Timothy with similar words (1 Tim. 6v12). He had fought against the Evil One (1 Thess. 2v18; Eph. 6v10-12), against the fallenness still within (Gal. 5v16) and the hostility of men, with the Lord's strength (Phil. 4v13; 2 Tim. 3v11; 4v16-17). *The Faith* – as a custodian of the truth Paul had kept what had been entrusted to him by God. Paul didn't compromise, desert or defect. Earlier in Antioch he was even willing to withstand Peter for the sake of the truth (Gal. 2v11f). He had guarded the deposit of revealed truth. *The Finish* – Paul had run a good race. The course was the course mapped out for him by his Lord. It is easy to start but the question is how do we finish? Sadly, in ministry many do not finish well. In the light of the challenge of this book perhaps you need to start again?

Now there was a crown, v8. Paul would be awarded a crown, not a laurel wreath, which would be awarded in the athletic contest (1Cor. 9v26), but an incorruptible crown which is the crown of righteousness. This crown is not so much the reward for Paul's holiness of living. The crown is the believer's full realisation of God's righteousness. The Emperor Nero may declare the apostle guilty and condemn him to death, but there will soon be a magnificent overturning of Nero's verdict, when the Lord, the righteous judge declares him righteous.

The apostle is quick to add that the crown is not a special reservation for himself alone. The same reward awaits 'all who love his appearing'. If you are an unbeliever you will dread it, but the believer should not fear it. He can be prepared for it if he truly lives as Paul had done, with the same sacrifice and submission to the will of God, the course God had mapped out for him.

The Final Movements v9-13 In these verses we are introduced to different members of Paul's 'missionary team'. We are reminded here of almost the 'roots' of a multi-ethnic, multi-cultural team which can be called upon to go on 'short-term' assignments as they are required – a very modern concept in mission!

Paul initially continues to address Timothy and urges him to lose no time in coming to him, (v9, 21). The request is similar to that of Tit. 3v12 with the adverb 'quickly' adding a note of urgency. This is in view of Paul's circumstances. The reason for the urgent request is because of what was happening with three members of Paul's team. Paul writes of the desertion of Demas. He is mentioned in Col. 4v14 and Phm. 24 as one of Paul's close associates who appears to have been fully involved in the work. Now tragically, we learn that he has 'deserted' Paul. The contrast between those who love Christ's appearing and those who love the present world is brought out. He has fallen in love with the values or the comforts of this present age. This is a big danger everywhere. Servants of the Lord, Cresens, mentioned only here in the NT, and Titus, are going in different directions, one to Galatia and the other to Dalmatia – as explained in Titus 3, the south western part of Illyricum – both to areas where Paul had previously engaged in Gospel work (Rom. 15v19). How available are we in the mission of God?

Luke was still there. He wants Mark to come; 'he is profitable to me' (v11). Precious evidence that when one fails miserably it is possible to start again and prove useful in God's work. See Acts 12v25; 13v13; 15v38, 39. Also Col. 4v10; Phm. 24; 1 Pet. 5v23. Mark overcame his earlier problems to develop into a dependable and 'useful' co-worker. Do you need to start again? God is the God of the second chance. Regarding Tychicus, he is probably the one to relieve Timothy and who takes this letter to him, (v12). All, apart from Demas were available. How is it with you?

The cloak, (v13) is a heavy outer garment, made normally from goat hair, hide or wool which often doubled as an outer protective garment to cover the owner while he slept. The cloak would keep him warm and 'the scrolls, especially the parchments' would keep him occupied. He wished to be busy to the end. **May God give us the same commitment! The mission of God continues!**

What Jesus Said John 9v4

In many ways Jesus spoke of mission – we think of the 'commissions' at the close of the Gospels e.g., Matt. 28v19-20. But I focus just on one verse where Jesus speaks about his commitment to mission, **John 9v4**, 'I must work the works of Him that sent me, while it is day: the night cometh, when no man can work'.

Here Jesus reveals his own involvement in the mission of God.

(1) It was **PERSONAL** Jesus said 'I' must work. He did not leave it to the angels/prophets – He took it on himself. He came to be involved. If Jesus could work why not you? In Col 4v11 Paul can write of his 'fellowworkers unto the kingdom of God, which have been a comfort' unto him. Would Paul approve of your level of commitment? What role do you play in the mission of God? There is something for you to do, somewhere for you to serve.

(2) It is **ESSENTIAL.** Note the use of 'must'. Here we have one of John's musts. Note the others – John 3v7; 3v14; 3v30; 4v24. If regeneration was essential, also the death of Christ, our growth in him and worship, his use of 'must' for kingdom work emphasises that our involvement in the mission of God is vitally important. We are left here to serve God, 1Cor.3v13.

(3) It is **SACRIFICIAL.** It was 'work'. To serve God is costly in time and effort. To be involved will mean sacrificing other things.

(4) It is **VOCATIONAL** 'Him that sent me'. We too are sent. We noted John 20v21 'As my father has sent me, even so send I you'.

(5) It is **TEMPORAL** 'while it is day: the night cometh, when no man can work'. The coming of the Lord is drawing near. In Acts 1v11 when Jesus ascended before the watching disciples the angels said 'Why stand ye gazing up into heaven? This same Jesus shall so come..'. In other words the angels were saying 'Why are you standing here looking up? Have you not just been given a work to do, a task to take the gospel to the world?' We still have that same task as the first disciples. The great Hymn says, 'Facing a task unfinished …'. In Romania – or wherever God's plan for you is.

I final word also has to be included, for any of you who are yet unsaved. Jesus has said here 'the night cometh when no man can work'. Elsewhere in the Scriptures in many places we read that the night is coming when your opportunity to be saved will be gone! I appeal to you that if God has been speaking to you through the testimony of this book, remember the words of Ps. 95v7-8, 'Today if ye will hear his voice, Harden not your heart'. You are a sinner, for the Bible says plainly, 'For all have sinned and come short of the glory of God', Rom.3v23. And Jesus has reminded us in John 8v21, you 'shall die in your sins: whither I go, ye cannot come'. You are SHUT OUT of heaven! You need to realise that you can do nothing to change this – no works, since Tit. 3v5 emphasises that salvation is 'not by works of righteousness which we have done'. Neither what you can pay, for Peter makes clear that his Christian readers 'were not redeemed with corruptible things as silver or gold' (1 Pet. 1v18). Nor will any religious ordinance in which you might participate change your relationship with God. In Acts 10v44-48 the congregation gathered in the home of Cornelius did not receive the Holy Spirit through baptism BUT were baptised BECAUSE the Spirit had already been poured out upon them! No, we can do nothing ourselves to get right with God.

Does this mean that there is NO HOPE? Praise God that the good news of the Gospel is that when we could do nothing GOD IN LOVE DID EVERYTHING. He gave his Son to die and pay the price for sinners. Everything that needs to be done for the sinner's acceptance has been done by Jesus on the cross – he cried 'It is finished!' (John 19v30). You must turn from your independence of God, where self has been on the throne of your heart, turn from your rebellion e.g., 'I will live my own life. Do what I wish to do, be what I wish to be'; turn to submit to him and trust alone for your acceptance in Christ and what he has accomplished on the cross. John also makes clear in 3v36, 'He that believeth on the Son hath everlasting life: and he that believeth not the Son shall not see life; but the wrath of God abideth on him'.

My book has the title, *By the Grace of God, I am what I am*. Since the moment God 'stopped' me when I was just over seventeen by the grace of God I have tried to go forward in submission to where I believe he would have me minister. Paul had a course, as do I. That path has taken me from a little village – Ballyhalbert – on the Ards Peninsula throughout Ireland, north and south and far beyond to preach in the major cities and towns of Romania, to teach the next generation of the 'army' of the Lord in Emanuel and to travel down some very minor roads – sometimes no roads at all but only mud tracks to bring the Good News of the gospel to ready listeners. An ever-open door is before me...

BIBLIOGRAPHY

Birnie, J., *Just Call me Paul*, (Slavic Gospel Association [UK], 2014).

Hendriksen, W., *I & II Timothy and Titus*, (London: The Banner of Truth Trust, 1972).

Liegeois, Jean-Pierre and Nicolae Gheorghe., *Roma/Gypsies: A European Minority*, (London: Minority Rights Group, 1995).

Koehl, R.L., *RKFDV: German Resettlement and Population Policy 1939-1945*, (Cambridge, MA: Harvard University Press, 1957).

Kuiper, R. B., *God Centred Evangelism: A Presentation of the Scriptural Theology of Evangelism*, (Edinburgh: Banner of Truth Trust, 1966).

Latourette, K. S., *A History of the Expansion of Christianity*, Vol. 1 *The First Five Centuries*, (New York: Harper & Brothers, 1937).

Lloyd-Jones, D. Martyn., *Preaching and Preachers*, (Grand Rapids, Michigan: Zondervan Publishing House, 1972).

The Christian Warfare: An Exposition of Ephesians 6v10-13, (Grand Rapids, MI, Baker Books, 1976).

Preaching and Preachers, (Grand Rapids, Michigan: Zondervan Publishing House, 1972).

Martin, A. N., *What's Wrong with Preaching Today?* (Edinburgh: Banner of Truth Trust, 1967).

Mills, B., *In Heavenly Love Abiding*, (Ballymena, The Pen & Quill, n.d.).

Moore, H., *1 & 2 Timothy and Titus: Missional Texts from a Great Missionary Statesman*, (Belfast: J.C. Print, 2016).

Mounce, W.D., *Pastoral Epistles*, Word Biblical Commentary, (Nashville: Thomas Nelson, 2000).

Orme, W., *The Practical Works of the Rev. Richard Baxter*, Vol. X1V, (London, James Duncan, 37, Paternoster Row, 1830).

Packer, J.I., *Evangelism and the Sovereignty of God* (Chicago: Inter Varsity Press, 1961).

Patton, W. J., *Pardon and Assurance: Being Addresses by the Rev. William J. Patton*, ed. Rev. John McIlveen, D.D., (Edinburgh & London: Oliphant Anderson & Ferrier, 1911).

Sabates-Wheeler, R., *Cooperation in the Romanian Countryside: an Insight into Post Soviet Agriculture* (Langham, Maryland: Lexington Books, 2005).

Schmidt, U., *Die Deutschen aus Bessarabien: eine Minderheit Südosteuropa (1814 bis heute)*, (Köln: Böhlau Verlag GmbH, 2004).

Sherwin-White, A.N., Roman Society and Roman Law in the New Testament, (Oxford: Clarendon, 1963).

Spurgeon, C. H., 'Household Salvation', A Sermon (No. 1019), Metropolitan Tabernacle Pulpit delivered on Lord's Day Morning, Nov. 15th 1871.

Stewart, J.S., *Thine is the Kingdom*, (New York: J. Scribner's Sons, 1956).

Stott, J. R. W., *Motives and Methods in Evangelism* (IVP Booklet, 1962).

Our Guilty Silence: The Church, the Gospel & the World, (London: Hodder & Stoughton, 1967).

Towner, P.H., *The Letters to Timothy and Titus*, The New International Commentary on the New Testament, (Grand Rapids: Wm. B Eerdmans Publishing Co., 2006).

Vashen, Y., 'Executive Summary: Historical Findings & Recommendations', (The International Commission on the Holocaust in Romania, Nov. 11 2004). (The Holocaust Martyr's & Heroes' Remembrance Authority).

Wenham, J. W., *The Elements of New Testament Greek*, (Cambridge: Cambridge University Press, 1965).

Wiles, M. F., *The Spiritual Gospel: The Interpretation of the Fourth Gospel in the Early Church*, (Cambridge: Cambridge University Press, 1960).

Wurmbrand, R., *Tortured for Christ*, (London: Hodder and Stoughton, 1967).

In God's Underground, (London: Hodder and Stoughton, 1968).

From Suffering to Triumph, (Kregel Publications, Grand Rapids, MI, 1991).

WEBSITES

www.thetravellingteam.org/articles/amy-carmichaels-dream accessed March 2016.
www.visitingromania.net accessed April 2016.

www.revisionist.net/german-expulsions.html accessed May 2016.

http://www.bessarabien.de/geschichte/auswanderung.htm accessed April 2016.

www.theguardian.com/news/2014/dec10 accessed May 2016.

www.ncregister.com/blog/signs-of-the-cross-in-romania-christianity-thrives-in-post-communist-country accessed May 2016.

https://en.wikipedia.org/wiki/Romania_in_World_War_11 accessed April 2016.

https://en.wikipedia.org/wiki/History-of-the-Jews-in-Romania accessed April 2016.

https://en.wikipedia.org/wiki/Romanian_People's_Tribunals accessed May 2016.

A nagyváradi „ver fényes magyar ünnep" (The "shiny Hungarian holiday" in Oradea), Erdélyi Napló, 4 February, 2009 accessed April 2016.

www.theguardian.com/news/ 2014/ dec10 accessed May 2016.

https://ro.wikipedia.org/wiki/Liviu_Olah accessed May 2016.

https://en.wikipedia.org/wiki/Religious_persecution_in_Communist_Romania accessed May 2016.
www.transformeuropenow.org/romania/casa-grace accessed May 2016.
www.internationaladoptionguide.co.uk/blog/views/ orphans-romania-history accessed May 2016.
www.emanuel.ro accessed April 2016.
www.transformeuropenow.org/romania/casa-grace accessed May 2016.

Clujmulticultural.ro/local-communities/romani-culture/pata-rat-community/ accessed May 2016.
ecmi.org/europe/country/ro/ accessed May 2016.
www.operationworld.org/roma accessed May 2016.

ENDNOTES

1. R. B. Kuiper, *God Centred Evangelism: A Presentation of the Scriptural Theology of Evangelism*, (Edinburgh: Banner of Truth Trust, 1966), p. 13 ff.

2. J. S. Stewart, *Thine is the Kingdom*, (New York: J. Scribner's Sons, 1956) pp.14-15.

3. K.S. Latourette, *A History of the Expansion of Christianity*, Vol. 1 *The First Five Centuries*, (New York: Harper & Brothers, 1937), p.117.

4. J. R. W. Stott, *Motives and Methods in Evangelism* (IVP Booklet, 1962), p.5.

5. J. R. W. Stott, *Our Guilty Silence: The Church, the Gospel & the World*, (London: Hodder & Stoughton, 1967), p. 20 f.

6. Stott, *Our Guilty Silence*, p. 28.

7. www.thetravellingteam.org/articles/amy-carmichaels-dream accessed March 2016.

8. W. J. Patton, *Pardon and Assurance: Being Addresses by the Rev. William J. Patton*, ed. Rev. John McIlveen, D.D., (Edinburgh & London: Oliphant Anderson & Ferrier, 1911).

9. Patton, 'The Wages of Sin', in *Pardon and Assurance: Being Addresses by the Rev. William J. Patton*, p. 90.

10. D. Martyn Lloyd-Jones, *Preaching and Preachers*, (Grand Rapids, Michigan: Zondervan Publishing House, 1972), p.92

11. A. N. Martin, *What's Wrong with Preaching Today?* (Edinburgh: Banner of Truth Trust, 1967), p.13.

12. See W. Orme, *The Practical Works of the Rev. Richard Baxter*, Vol. X1V, (London, James Duncan, 37, Paternoster Row, 1830), p. 182.

13. D. Martyn Lloyd Jones, *The Christian Warfare: An Exposition of Ephesians 6v10-13*, (Grand Rapids, MI, Baker Books, 1976), p.273.

14. Lloyd-Jones, *Preaching and Preachers*, p.91.

15   Lloyd-Jones, *Preaching and Preachers*, p.71 ff.

16   C. H. Spurgeon, Metropolitan Tabernacle Pulpit, 'Household Salvation', A Sermon (No. 1019) delivered on Lord's Day Morning, Nov. 15th 1871.

17   H Moore, *1 & 2 Timothy and Titus: Missional Texts from a Great Missionary Statesman*, (Belfast: J. C Print, 2016), p. 64.

18   J.I. Packer, *Evangelism and the Sovereignty of God* (Chicago: Inter Varsity Press, 1961), p.65ff.

19   B. Mills, *In Heavenly Love Abiding*, (Ballymena, The Pen & Quill, n.d.), p. 18.

20   Mills, *In Heavenly Love Abiding*, p.20-21.

21   J. W. Wenham, *The Elements of New Testament Greek*, (Cambridge: Cambridge University Press, 1965).

22   In M.F. Wiles, *The Spiritual Gospel: The Interpretation of the Fourth Gospel in the Early Church*, (Cambridge: Cambridge University Press, 1960), p.8.

23   Moore, *1 & 2 Timothy and Titus: Missional Texts from a Great Missionary Statesman*, p.236-237.

24   Slavic Gospel Association was initially founded by Peter Deyneka in 1934 a Russian emigrant to the USA with its first British Council meeting (SGA UK) in 1950. During the 70s the mission responded to specific requests from local church pastors in Eastern Europe to provide structured courses to be taught in secret locations to groups of potential leaders. In the late 80's there were seven groups meeting across Romania. SGA (UK) is now one of five international offices which are autonomous but together work with Slavic peoples, the others concentrating mainly in the C.I.S. (the former Soviet Union).

25   www.visitingromania.net accessed April 2016.

26   R. Sabates-Wheeler, *Cooperation in the Romanian Countryside: an Insight into Post Soviet Agriculture* (Langham, Maryland: Lexington Books, 2005) p.5.

27   http://www.bessarabien.de/geschichte/auswanderung.htm accessed: April 2016; U. Schmidt, Die Deutschen aus Bessarabien: eine Minderheit Südosteuropa (1814 bis heute), (Köln: Böhlau Verlag GmbH, 2004), p. 72

28   R. L. Koehl, *RKFDV: German Resettlement and Population Policy 1939-1945*, (Cambridge, MA: Harvard University Press, 1957), p.254.

29   See Victor Gaetan, in www.ncregister.com/blog/signs-of-the-cross-in-romania-christianity-thrives-in-post-communist-country accessed May 2016.

30   www.revisionist.net/german-expulsions.html

31   https://en.wikipedia.org/wiki/Romania_in_World_War_11 accessed April 2016.

32   https://en.wikipedia.org/wiki/History-of-the-Jews-in-Romania accessed April 2016.

33   https://en.wikipedia.org/wiki/Romanian_People's_Tribunals accessed May 2016.

34   Yad Vashen, 'Executive Summary: Historical Findings & Recommendations', (The International Commission on the Holocaust in Romania Nov. 11, 2004), (The Holocaust Martyrs' & Heroes' Remembrance Authority).

35   The Second Vienna Award was the second of two territorial disputes arbitrated by Nazi Germany and Fascist Italy. Rendered on 30 August 1940, it reassigned the territory of Northern Transylvania (including all of Maramures and part of Crisana) from Romania to Hungary.

36   A nagyváradi „ver fényes magyar ünnep" (The "shiny Hungarian holiday" in Oradea), Erdélyi Napló, 4 February, 2009 accessed April 2016.

37   Liegeois, Jean-Pierre and Nicolae Gheorghe, *Roma/Gypsies: A European Minority*, (London: Minority Rights Group, 1995). In some cases estimates are considerably higher than official figures, due at least partly to the reluctance of some Roma to identify themselves as such.

38   Viorel Achim, T*he Roma in Romanian History,* Trans by Richard Davies, (Budapest: Central European University Press, 2004), p.203.

39   Clujmulticultural.ro/local-communities/romani-culture/pata-rat-community/ accessed May 2016

40   There are very differing estimates of the number of children in state institutions. See Vlad Odobescu, 'An Insight into Romanian Orphan History', Jan. 4, 2016, in www.internationaladoptionguide.co.uk/blog/views/orphans-romania-history accessed May 2016.

41   See the 2014 article by Wendell Steavenson, 'Ceausescu's Children', in www.theguardian.com/news/ 2014/ dec10 accessed May 2016.

42   www.transformeuropenow.org/romania/casa-grace accessed May 2016.

43 R. Wurmbrand, *Tortured for Christ*, (London: Hodder and Stoughton, 1967), p.13.

44 Note the spelling in the quotation used by Wurmbrand. In English, the name of the country was formerly spelled Rumania. Romania became the predominant spelling around 1975. Romania is also the official English-language spelling used by the Romanian government.

45 Occasionally word would get out to his family that he was still alive, either through a 'secret disciple' who was part of the communist regime or someone being released e.g., a girl in the truck from his church (extreme poverty had turned her to theft and she had been imprisoned but was about to be freed) as he was being moved because of his tuberculosis from Vacaresti to Tirgul–Ocna where the prison had a sanatorium of sorts. See R. Wurmbrand, *In God's Underground*, (London: Hodder and Stoughton, 1968), p.72-73.

46 Wurmbrand, *Tortured for Christ*, p.34.

47 Wurmbrand, *Tortured for Christ*, p.52.

48 Wurmbrand, *With God in Solitary Confinement*, (Bartlesville, OK: Living Sacrifice Book Company, 1969).

49 Wurmbrand wrote, 'We continued the *underground* work of the *Underground* Church in *underground* communist prisons', *Tortured for Christ*, p.39.

50 See Wurmbrand, *Tortured for Christ*, p.32.

51 The report of Wurmbrand's 1996 interview about his fourteen-year imprisonment in Romania. See https://en.wikipedia.org/wiki/Religious_persecution_in_Communist_Romania accessed May 2016.

52 Wurmbrand, *In God's Underground*, p. 62-63.

53 Wurmbrand, *In God's Underground*, p. 62.

54 Wurmbrand, *In God's Underground*, p.64.

55 See Wurmbrand, *In God's Underground*, p.167.

56 R. Wurmbrand, *From Suffering to Triumph*, (Kregel Publications, Grand Rapids, MI, 1991), p.11.

57 See www.emanuel.ro accessed April 2016.

58 BEE refers to the mission Bible Education by Extension which was founded in 1979 when initially five Missions plus a number of key national leaders

working in Eastern Europe put together a training programme for those who would become church leaders behind the Iron Curtain. The mission now has grown to become BEE World with 50,000 students in 15 countries who take the BEE courses.

59 J. Birnie, *Just Call me Paul*, (Slavic Gospel Association (UK) Ltd., 2014), p.127.

60 The summary here is taken mainly from https://ro.wikipedia.org/wiki/Liviu_Olah accessed May 2016. See also Paul Negrut's commendation of him in Birnie, *Just Call me Paul*, p. 58-65.

61 Birnie, *Just Call me Paul*, p.56.

62 Birnie, *Just Call me Paul*, p. 105.

63 Birnie, *Just Call me Paul*, p. 131-132.

64 An unreformed Church that separated from Rome in the Great Schism of the 11th century over the Filioque, the procession of the Holy Spirit from the Father *and* from the Son, which Orthodoxy denies. Figures of Church numbers are taken from ecmi.org/europe/country/ro/ and www.operationworld.org/roma accessed May 2016.

65 They are published on our blog http://tellromania.wordpress.com.

66 Moore, *1 & 2 Timothy and Titus: Missional Texts from a Great Missionary Statesman*, p.71, 184, 220, 236.

67 Matthew Henry, Commentary on the Whole Bible, vol. VI (accessed November 2012).